180°

To Salvation

ISBN 978-0-557-49051-6

I would like to thank God for giving me the ability to be able to share my testimony with the world. I want to thank everyone along the way that has helped me in the building of my faith. I want to thank everyone that is mentioned in my book and to those that were not mentioned but still had an impact on my life. I truly have been blessed to be in the position that I am in to be able to share my story. I want to thank the Lord for urging me to write my inspirational story so that it may help others who read it. I want to thank my mother and father for raising me to be who I am today and a special thanks to my mother who helped with the editing of the book. Lastly but most importantly I would like to send a lifetime of thank you's to my wife who not only supported me through everything but is an inspiration to me. I am so lucky to have married an angel sent to me from above who is not only my loving partner for life but my best friend as well.

Humble yourselves before the Lord, and he will lift you up

-James 4:10

1

The Early Years

As I look back at my childhood I can remember certain little things that would have ties to being religious, but we were far from a religious family. Bits and pieces here and there such as a nativity set put out for Christmas or an ornament that my brother had made of baby Jesus in the manger hung on the tree. Little subtleties that might give an appearance of Christianity being prcsent in thc houschold, but far from a blatant display. Thc onc thing that does stand out in my mind was that my brother and I did attend a Presbyterian School. I went to the school from preschool until second grade, before we moved away. I was too young to know what my parents reasoning for putting us in that school was. I think that if you asked them today they would tell you it had more to do with the fact that public schools were a little rougher than it had to do with any religious experience. It was a mystery because nothing outside of school was ever geared towards Christianity. For whatever the reason, I am thankful today that they did place me in the Presbyterian school, because it was at that school where the foundation of Christianity was laid for me.

I was born on December 17th 1979 to Bob and Barbara Wheeler. I am a middle child with an older brother, Scott, and a younger sister, Melissa. My father was an only child raised in southern California with no religious affiliation. My mother on the other hand was one of four children also raised in southern California, but my grandparents would attend church on a regular basis. Both of my parents are very caring people and were the best parents a kid could ever have growing up. Both of them are very intelligent people, my mother is a believer and lays her trust in the Lord while my father is a non-believer who relies heavily on science when it comes to the talk of creation.

While attending Valley Presbyterian School it must have been mandatory that each child was to have their own Bible because I remember having my own Bible when I was younger. In my mind I can picture two different Bibles, I think one was mine and one was Scott's, but we shared everything so it is hard to differentiate whose was whose. One of the Bibles had a red cover and the words Holy Bible etched in gold lettering on it, while the other was cream colored with a picture of Jesus holding a sheep. Both of these were picture Bibles for children that only scratched the surface of what the Bible was actually about. These Bibles were intended to get across the main themes and important figures in the Bible while simplifying everything with pictures.

As a student I learned things that I was not taught at home such as how to pray and who the main figures in the Bible were. I don't remember if I asked questions about God or religion at home, but if I don't remember these things than religion outside of school must not have played an important role in our household.

While growing up I would do normal activities that kids do, I would also get into trouble a little bit, but nothing too serious. I loved baseball and I loved playing baseball with my brother Scott. I watched TV every afternoon when I came home from school the cartoon G.I Joe or the shows "Emergency" and "CHiPs" were my favorites. I also loved to color or draw and I absolutely loved playing with my toys. Star Wars and G.I Joe's were my favorites. My brother and I were best friends at this age and did everything together; we played cops and robbers, rode our bikes and played bascball until we were worn out.

I liked school and had some friends from my elementary class but I couldn't wait for the weekend to come. I would wake up early on weekend mornings, sometimes earlier than I would have to during the week, and retreat to our playroom. In the playroom I would turn on the TV to a cartoon station and begin bringing out my toys to play. I would build forts with blocks or set up all of our "Hot Wheels" to recreate a city scene, I enjoyed my weekend mornings. Around nine or ten in the morning my parents would wake up and make us breakfast, the smell of bacon or pancakes would fill the house. I loved being outdoors as well and after breakfast Scott and I would spend the better part of the day outside playing. I had a very vivid imagination and was the kind of kid who liked to play with others but also had fun playing alone because of my great ability to pretend.

Outside of my home I was exposed to religion by other people such as my grandparents and my aunt and uncle. When at my grandparent's house I can remember my grandpa sitting down with me and whoever else was around to read passages from the Bible to us. Not only did my grandpa read from the Bible both him and my grandma would reinforce themes from the Bible.

My aunt Yoli, Uncle David and their three children would attend church every Sunday. When my brother, sister and I would stay at their house we would attend church with them. I was not old enough to attend church services so I would go with my cousin Mark to his Sunday school class. These classes would be filled with activities to learn messages from the Bible. While at my Uncle's house we would always have prayer before each meal to thank God for providing the food for us and to give thanks for other blessings in our everyday lives.

Before we went to bed my Uncle would gather us around and read a passage from the Bible and go over it with us. He would ask us questions to make sure that we understood the message and how it applied to our lives. I remember that I always liked these group sessions, but was always nervous about being called on to answer the questions. I felt that if I got the answer wrong or did not know the answer that it made me somehow less in the eyes of God.

When I was about twelve years old I would go with my grandpa on his selling rounds. He worked as a salesman for Brown and Bigelow selling anything that was capable of putting a business' name on it. Most of his sales came in the form of calendars and pens. I would ride in the passenger seat of his late eighties maroon Honda Accord while he told jokes and stories.

Whenever we went inside a place of business to speak to the owner about an order my grandpa would always put me on the spot with some trick that I could do. At the time I remember feeling embarrassed when he would tell a complete stranger that I was on my way to becoming a Major League pitcher or that I could juggle. But now looking back I feel a warm feeling inside knowing that my grandpa was proud enough of me and my accomplishments that he could brag about them to almost complete strangers.

Some of the stories that my grandpa would tell me were about his time as a Gideon. Gideon's are evangelical Protestant organization dedicated to distributing copies of the Bible in over 80 languages and 190 countries of the world to those who might not otherwise encounter it, most famously in hotel and motel rooms. He would tell me about his trips up to the boy's juvenile hall and how he would pass out these Bibles to help kids turn there lives around.

Another influence on me as I grew up was my Uncle Roger. Roger had been stricken with Cerebral Palsy and mental retardation from contracting encephalitis as a baby. Even though his condition affected his mind and his motor skills it never affected his faith. Roger was always singing gospel songs and talking about the baby Jesus. Roger's biggest claim to fame was his pre-meal prayers. Even though his prayer only consisted of seven words it had the power to bring a smile to everyone's face in the room. His prayer went like this "For God's grace, and God's love, Amen."

My family moved to Palmdale from the San Fernando Valley when I was in fourth grade. I liked the move because we had a much larger, two story home. I also liked the fact that I was allowed out in the neighborhood more due to the fact that it was a much safer neighborhood then the one we came from. I was enjoying life like any kid does at this age, oblivious to the real world around them. I knew what was in my immediate world around me and not much else.

After moving farther away from my cousins we were unable to visit as much so we took up writing letters to each other. When I was in the sixth grade I remember writing letters back and forth to my cousin Mark. These letters would contain some Bible verses that Mark had gone over in his classroom; he attended a private Christian school. I would look these verses up and read them to myself. Sometimes he would send handouts that he was given in class or he would send me drawings that he had done. I remember a drawing that he sent me one time that had a picture of Jesus on the cross and next to the drawing had big block letters spelling out Jesus. Unfortunately this only lasted for about six months before, for whatever reason, we just stopped writing each other.

All the way up through high school I can only remember attending church a couple of times. One of those times was for an Easter service while I was down at my aunt and uncle's house. We went to a minor league baseball stadium in Rancho Cucamonga. Other than that I don't remember having any real ties with the church or religion period.

I was just wandering through life without any real destination. I had a few relationships and many friends throughout this time but no one I knew had a relationship with

God. It is sad to say but religion never really came up or at least didn't do anything to grab my attention. I say this is sad because God's glory is in and around us everyday and everywhere. A person can't go through life and not see all of God's works, unless the person is forcing themselves to see something different.

I had been playing baseball my entire life and now that I was a junior in high school I decided to try out for the team. Up until the tryout I had only played in little league, but I was better than most of the kids my age so I thought I had a pretty good chance of making the team. I ended up making the team and baseball would turn out to be what God chose for me to experience to make his point later in life. I was really good at baseball but just like with life I really didn't have any direction or guidance. I look back and realize that with a little help I could have been even better. I did pretty well my junior season and was having fun pitching and hitting. I met some friends through baseball that were better than any other friends I had due to the sole fact that we had baseball in common.

The next year as a senior I was being looked upon to carry the team with my pitching. I was noted in the newspaper by my coach and big things were expected. I did very well for a pretty poor team and was even taught a few life lessons from my coach. I had trouble throughout my life being serious about situations. I had a comfort zone in humor and always turned to it when I was seeking attention. One of my biggest problems was that I didn't know how to draw the line between being serious and being comical. I would constantly push things too far and that is where I would get into trouble. I used the reasoning that if a little bit was funny then a truckload would be hilarious.

I also was having the problem that I didn't know how to do things on my own so I just took whatever fell in my lap. For example, while playing in an all-star game for local high school players I was approached by the local community college coach. He asked me if I would like to come play for his team. I said sure, because I had nothing else that I was planning on doing. I was excited to continue to play the game that I loved so much but I was oblivious to other options or schools.

I went out to practices for Antelope Valley College over the summer but found out that it was too time consuming for me and quit. I found a job instead at Pizza Hut as a delivery driver and was happy making money. I started going to college but was doing poorly for the first couple of semesters because I was not feeling any pressure to do well. I had been groomed by my parents over a long period of time to respond to rewards, I rarely, if ever, did anything without expecting something. I had no drive inside to accomplish goals because I didn't see the importance in it for me. I didn't have a lot of foresight into where my future was headed.

After two years of the same thing, going to school and working at Pizza Hut, I was getting bored not to mention having no direction in school. One night I was coming back from the San Fernando Valley, with my girlfriend at the time, and it was raining pretty hard. I was driving my 1996 Chevy Camaro RS when all of a sudden I could feel the car lose traction for a split second. This scared me and I decided that I needed to get off of the freeway to stay the night at my grandparent's house.

I was in the far right lane so that I could take the exit towards my grandparent's house when the back end of the card lost total traction. The car began to fishtail and I panicked. I pressed on the brake and turned the wheel which caused the car to go into an out of control spin. The car spun across four lanes of traffic out of control. It did a complete three-sixty and another half of one before slamming into the center median. The car ended up sticking half way out into the fast lane of traffic facing the wrong way. Luckily enough for us no cars hit us during this ordeal and within thirty seconds of the accident there was a highway patrol officer on scene.

Nobody was hurt in the accident and I was extremely shaken up. I still get nervous driving in the rain to this day. The car being wrecked allowed for my parents to purchase a 2001 Pontiac Firebird for me. I didn't want to drive this around as a pizza delivery driver so I was forced to find a new job and quickly found a job at a well known electronics store.

While working for the electronic store I got into the bad habit of stealing. I worked in the computer department and others employees would bring over music CD's for us to burn a few copies for other employees. I had all of the latest CD's and they were all free. One day I was asked to set up a display for a brand new hot video game called Warcraft 2. I set up the display and at the end of the weekend I took the display down. The video game I took out of the computer should have been returned to the department but instead I put it into my pocket. I quickly went on my break so that I could take it out to my car. After depositing the game in my car I turned around went back to work and never gave it another thought.

I had the next couple of days off from work but when I returned I was busted immediately. I came in for my shift and didn't think anything was up. Boy was I wrong. I was approached by a manager and was sat down in a conference room. I was told that we could do this the easy way or the hard way, as the manager said this he revealed a video surveillance tape. I told him the easy way for sure. The manager told me that I would only be suspended if I brought in the stolen disc. When I brought in the disc the manager was nice enough to tell me to quit otherwise I would be fired while I was on suspension.

I quit my job at the electronic store where I had worked for only a year. I lied to my parents and told them that I quit because they were not giving me enough hours. I found a job quickly at a brand new store opening up down the street from my house which was a sporting goods store.

This was going to be a new opportunity for me and I was not going to fall into the same bad habits that had plagued me before or so I thought. I had been stealing for a long time before the electronic store incident. One time I remember opening a pack of football cards in a store and pulling out a 1991 card of Jeff George and placing it down into my underpants. This was the first time I had ever stolen anything in a public store, before I had just taken a couple of my friend's baseball cards when they were not looking.

The real thievery began when a friend of my brother's showed me how to steal from the guys who owned the local baseball card store. The two elderly gentlemen who owned and ran the card store were not perceptive enough to pick up on my slick tricks. I remember when the baseball card store closed it was a sad day, but I felt a little responsible for the closing because I had stolen so much over the years.

During this time I was playing a lot of softball but had not played any baseball since high school. One day my brother Scott approached me and asked me if I wanted to play in an adult baseball league on the weekends. I agreed and started playing for the Waves in the San Fernando area. I was by far the best player on our team; I was a very dominant pitcher in the league as well. Our team made the championship game but lost to a team comprised of much younger and more talented players. Although the team was comprised of mostly older not as talented players I had a lot of fun playing on the same team as my brother.

While finishing up my classes at Antelope Valley College I decided that I was going to get my degree in teaching. I planned on transferring to Cal State University of Bakersfield, but would be attending their satellite program located on the AVC campus. I started my classes which were Economics, Linguistics and English. It was a different experience but after one quarter I was told that I was missing statistics and could not continue on without that class. This meant that I had to go back to Antelope Valley College for one single class, what a waste of time.

My girlfriend at the time suggested that I go out for the baseball team while I was taking the one class that I needed. I decided that I would give it a try and go talk to the coach to find out if I could tryout. I approached the coach, Jeffrey Leonard, who was a retired major league baseball player that I knew all about as a kid. He is a very intimidating looking man and asked me a series of questions about what positions I played. When I told him that I was a pitcher he asked me how fast I threw, so I told him about eighty miles an hour. In fact I had no idea. He told me that I could come for a tryout the very next day.

The next day I played with the team and thought I did pretty well but I was always hard on myself. Coach Leonard who went by the name “Hac” pulled me aside and told me I had made the team. He told me to go enroll in the baseball class for next semester and to make sure that I had at least twelve units to make me eligible for the season. This was a very exciting and happy day for me. I knew that this was going to be good experience and a good opportunity for me, I just didn’t know how good at the time.

2

College Baseball

College baseball at Antelope Valley College was a huge step for me. This program was on the rise and I didn't have the luxury of playing summer or even fall ball with the guys on the team. I came in over the winter and bonded quickly with some of the guys. The brothers Tyler and Jared Bain were two of my close friends along with Chase Dominguez, Phillip Seston and Greg Culver. Who were all very talented in their own regard.

Tyler was about 6'2, 240 pounds and had good velocity on his pitches to go along with some power at the plate. His younger brother Jared was a little bit taller than Tyler but weighed about twenty pounds lighter. Jared was a pretty good middle relief pitcher and later became a good hitting first baseman. Chase threw the ball the hardest reaching 90-92 mph but his control was the biggest problem. He never quite knew where the ball would end up. This was a problem he had encountered due to an accident which crushed both of his hands. He needed many surgeries to get him back to playing the game. Phil Seston was a man-child who had very strong hands and hit the ball harder than anyone I have ever seen. Seston one time made a metal bat explode just by hitting a baseball and hit some of the farthest home runs I have ever witnessed. Greg was a second baseman with lots of speed and everything he did on and off the field he did with style.

There were many differences about this team from any other team that I ever played on. This team was looked at like a bunch of thugs by other schools in the area. We used a lot of profanity on the field, mostly by the coach, and we carried ourselves in a manner that was a little rough around the edges. Although chewing tobacco was banned by the league most guys did it secretly or if you were a pitcher you did it while you weren't playing, usually in the dugout. Chew was used all the time during practice, on the bus rides to and from the games, and during class.

Another difference was the fact that we practiced all the time, five days a week, through the summer break and through the winter break. Not only were we practicing, we were playing all the time as we had a thirty two game schedule. This schedule was almost twice as many games than in high school and about three times as many games than I had played the year before in the adult league. I was eating, sleeping and breathing baseball. Practice and playing games six days a week along with all of the travel time. I was completely consumed by the game.

I found out early on that chewing tobacco was the cool thing to do for baseball players. I had never tried it before but was open to trying new things at this stage in my life. I remember I went into a gas station and pondered my decision between all of the different brands and flavors before deciding on a can of Kodiak Ice. I should have tried it at home but I waited until I reached the field before I opened up the can. Once opened the smell was very strong and would deter almost any beginner but I went for it anyways. I pinched what I thought was a good amount from the can and placed it in between my bottom lip and gums. Wow! I couldn't believe how strong this stuff was. Not only did it burn my gums but it made me so light headed that I was unsure if I could take the field. It didn't seem to matter. All I was worried about at the time was how to look cool doing it and being able to fit in with the other guys who did it.

Along with on the field bad habits I also picked up bad habits off the field as well such as, partying, smoking and consuming large quantities of alcohol. These were never a part of my life before I became a member of the AVC baseball team. I attributed it to being cool with the friends I had. I am not sure what my parents thought of my behavior, I am sure they knew about it even though I went to great lengths to keep them hidden. I would drench my self in cologne when returning home to cover up the smell of cigarettes and I would give no details about my whereabouts just that I was hanging out with friends.

Road trips for away games were always fun. No matter if we won or lost the team would always stop at a liquor store and pickup alcohol for the ride back home. Not only did the coach allow this he drank as well. He became more like one of the guys on the team than he was a coach. That is why some of the guys crossed the line when it came time for him to coach. Sometimes there were gray areas and it was hard to tell where that line between coach and friend was drawn.

The first year I did exceptionally well as a pitcher. I ended the year with four wins and only one loss while posting a decent earned run average. I was named "Pitcher of the Year" by my teammates at the end of the year. I had fun all season long and even was able to finish all that I needed for my Associates Degree in Letters, Arts and Sciences. I was thankful for the opportunity to play on the team and had my sights set on bigger and better things for the following season.

During the off season Chase and I decided that we would better our chances to continue playing after AVC baseball if we worked out hard over the summer. We came to the conclusion that we didn't want small results towards our next season we wanted drastic changes. So we decided that we were going to take steroids to help boost our workouts. I arranged to meet a guy that was a friend of a friend. I met him in a Carl's Jr parking lot and exchanged four hundred dollars cash for a brown paper bag. Inside the bag were enough steroids to last me and Chase for six weeks.

That summer my girlfriend at the time broke up with me and I began partying all of the time. Chase, Tyler and I would go to a club called Larue on Tuesday nights for dollar drink night and then to Schooner's on Wednesday nights for ladies night. Then on the weekends we would go to house parties all over the valley. This partying didn't stop when school started back up again either. When my sophomore season started we slowed down a bit but were still partying way too much.

Chase and I thought that with our workouts and steroid combination we would be throwing a lot harder when the season started. Truth is we both only threw about one to two miles an hour faster. The drastic changes that I was hoping for never appeared. The money wasted on the steroids and the chance of destroying my body was not worth the risk. Our fall ball season started off with a bang and our team looked primed and ready to go. I felt and looked good in my three starts in the fall, I couldn't wait for the season to open. I was dreaming of becoming a star in the league, winning awards and making the newspaper whenever I pitched.

The season came and I started having problems immediately. I was failing miserably and it couldn't have come at a worse time. This was my chance at getting an offer to play at a four year school and I was blowing it. I couldn't get out of my bad start to the season, things just kept getting worse. The harder I tried the worse the outcome. I couldn't understand why things were falling apart and the worst part about it was baseball was becoming not so much fun anymore.

During the season I was still working part time at the sporting goods store at night and on the weekends. I had fallen into the trap of reverting back to my stealing days. I am not sure if there was any correlation between my poor play on the field. It got to a point to where I actually looked forward to going to work so that I could steal some more stuff. I mostly stole clothing for sports called Under Armor and batting gloves. I would take these things and sell them either to guys on my team at a discounted price or on EBay.

Since the sporting goods store was not a big store there would only be one manager, one cashier and one salesperson closing up the store at night. When the manager would call the cashier into his office to count the money, I would begin. I knew how to maneuver around so that I wouldn't be spotted by the two security cameras. I would take the merchandise with me back to the backroom where there were no cameras at all. Once in this room I would tape the batting gloves to the insides of my calves under my pants with masking tape. My pants were baggy enough to disguise this type of concealment. If I was taking the Under Armor I would put the clothing on underneath my work clothes. This is where the dress code of the store benefited me greatly in my stealing practices, the dress code was a long sleeve button up shirt and a tie. No one every suspected anything, so the stealing continued.

The only time that I thought that I might get caught was when I got greedy one time. I was stealing Nike football gloves and selling them on EBay for about twenty-five dollars a piece. The only problem was that I stole too many of them and made it noticeably bare on the display rack. I stole about fifteen pairs of the gloves and coupled with the fact that they were a hot seller the store sold out. Whoever was doing inventory never ordered anymore because in the computer it still showed that we had fifteen pairs even though their were no more physically in the store.

I loved the fact that I could make more money by selling the stolen goods on EBay or to teammates than I was with my paycheck. I became paranoid a few times and thought that the store management was on to me but it didn't stop me. I continued all the way up until my last day of work. I had become so bold that in fact on my last day I somehow coerced the manager to look the other way when a couple of my friends walked out with some nice baseball gloves.

Not only was my on the field season bad and my life outside of baseball but my off the field baseball decisions were even worse. I was suspended from the team two times and yelled at a few more times. Ultimately I was thrown off the team for horsing around on a bus ride back from an away game. The poor kid I was wrestling with ended up tearing a ligament in his knee and have to have surgery. I ended the season with no wins and three losses, all of them bad, and an earned run average around fifteen. Outside of baseball I was partying, drinking and smoking a lot to try and drown out the bad things happening in my life. I was also fooling around with a few different girls that I met through school, work or at bars.

I was so far away from God at this point in my life that it is amazing that I ever made it to where I am today. I was looking for trouble wherever I could find it. I really wasn't thinking straight at this point. A lot of my ideas were not well thought out and I was living on the edge doing things without the fear of consequences. Plain and simply put I was lost, in every aspect of my life. I can remember one time I went to a party with some friends and I actually took my gun with me in my waistband. I was so full of stupid ideas and plans that were not well thought out. It is sad to recall these times.

This was a period of my life where I was living for the moment. I was enjoying all of the things that were detrimental to my life. I was drinking, smoking and chewing tobacco more than ever along with my bad eating and sleeping habits. I even tried smoking Marijuana under pressure from my peers a couple of times. Thank God that I didn't like it and only smoked it a handful of times. My life was in a downward spiral and I didn't even know it, the sad thing is that this was just the beginning.

Shortly after I was kicked off the baseball team I was given a recruiting form by Hac for a small private school out in Nebraska. I filled out the form and sent it back to the baseball coach really never giving it much thought. I was also talking with a few other coaches for small private schools not exactly what I had hoped for at the beginning of the season. At this point these schools were my only option; I knew that a bigger school would never waste their time with me.

Not only was I involved in some bad things I was surrounding myself with people that were not very good influences. I had a friend who was friends with a drug dealer. I made the mistake of accompanying this friend over to the dealer's house a couple of times and felt way out of my element but wanted to fit in at all costs. There were a couple of other guys in the house and all of them were smoking Marijuana. The dealer had a pit bull that was the biggest pit bull I had ever seen; the dog must have weighed almost a hundred and fifty pounds.

At one point the dealer asked me to take a hit out of his bong, I declined. He took this as being disrespectful towards him and told me that if I did not smoke then he would open the sliding door and have the dog attack me. I was now scared because everyone else in the room was high and laughing about what this guy was threatening me with. The dealer had a straight look on his face and he asked me again. I told him with fear in my voice that I didn't want to. He slid open the door just enough for the dog to stick his enormous head inside the house. I started telling him that this wasn't funny anymore. He just ignored me and began antagonizing the dog to make him angry. I didn't know if I should run out the door or stay in my seat. Finally out of no where the dealer closed the door and turned to me laughing. He told me that if I didn't want any I didn't have to have any. I never returned to that man's house again.

Another instance that blows my mind to look back on was a trip to Las Vegas I had with some friends. Chase was celebrating his twenty-first birthday with his friend Nick in Las Vegas. I decided with a couple of friends that were on the baseball team to make the trip to Vegas. We all piled into my Firebird around eight at night for the four hour trip. The funny part was seeing two six foot guys squeeze in the back seats of the car for the trip.

About half way through our trip one of the guys pulls out some cocaine. I had never seen cocaine in real life before and was blown away that it was in my car. I told the guys that whatever they were going to do with it they needed to hurry up and get rid of it. All of the guys did lines of the cocaine off of one of the guy's notebook from school. When all the lines were gone the little bit that remained was sprinkled into an unwrapped cigarette. Once the cigarette was lit I remember the very sweet smell of the smoke that it produced, almost like candy. I didn't want to have anything to do with such a powerful drug as cocaine and thankfully no one started pressuring me. I am so glad that I didn't try it that night because things might have turned out very differently if I had. Although I was doing a lot of stupid things at this time in my life I still had enough common sense to do the right thing in this situation.

During all of these turbulent times I was still in search of where I was going to attend school to further my education. My recruiting had begun and I sent out some emails and filled out some applications for only a very select few small private schools. Looking back I was so ill prepared in the process of continuing my education after AVC. I should have started the process at the beginning of my sophomore season not when there was two weeks left in the semester.

I sought out information on the following small schools, Azusa Pacific, Dana College, William Penn University and Bethany College. Azusa Pacific was a nice school that was close to home but I was never able to get in contact with anyone so it was the first to fall off the list. I was able to speak with and set up a recruiting trip for Bethany College and I even was able to get Chase to go along with me, which is when the fun began.

We left on a Friday, mid-morning for a four and a half hour drive up north from the Antelope Valley. We arrived and were met by the coach and assistant coach, who both invited us into the dining hall for dinner. While we were eating both of the coaches were telling us about all of the opportunities and all Bethany had to offer us. I am not sure if they were telling me and Chase things to scare us off or to make sure that this was really something that we wanted to commit too. The coach told us that every one of the 350 kids who attended Bethany College were required to go to chapel at 8:00 am every morning of the week. They told us how there were no alcoholic beverages on campus and absolutely no members of the opposite sex in our rooms at any time.

Then came the information about the baseball team, no chewing tobacco and no cussing on or off the field. We were told that the team had a practice field up on top a hill near the school and that the games were played down the street at the city park. The head coach offered us a dorm room to stay with a couple of players but we opted to stay at a nearby hotel instead. The coach told us to come back in the morning at 6:30 am for a chance to showcase our talent. In parting he told us that Bethany is a fabulous school and that this would be the place we would meet our future wives, because both of them did.

We went out drinking that night and met some girls from a sorority. We brought them back to stay in our hotel that night. Both of us didn’t like all of the rules that were going to be imposed on us when we were so used to doing whatever we wanted. This stage of our lives was meant to be wild and crazy not for forcing us to go to church.

We didn't like too many of the rules and the team didn't sound very good. But this was an opportunity to continue playing baseball while pursuing an education, and we both understood that we would be absolute studs in this league. With my pitching and Chase's hitting and pitching we would absolutely dominate this league and become legends in the making. That being said we both came to the agreement that it depended on how much money the coach was willing to offer us that would make up our mind. If the coach was willing to offer us a full ride scholarship on a $16,000 a year education then we couldn't pass that up, so we would just wait and see.

The next morning we woke up tired, as we did a little drinking in the hotel room the night before. We met up with the coach in our baseball attire and headed up the hill to the practice field. When we arrived at the practice field both Chase and I looked at each other in a look that could be summed up by, you have got to be kidding me. This practice field consisted of a flat grass and dirt field surrounded by a couple of hills and a forest. There was no field; it only existed in your imagination, no bases, no batter's box and certainly no pitcher's mound. The only thing that resembled anything to do with baseball was a rickety old enclosed batting cage. Next to the batting cage was a sorry excuse for a mound that looked more like a horse shoe pit.

Now it was time to perform, we both hit in the cage, if the talent pool was low then I was probably going to be asked to hit on an everyday basis. Then the pitching. My mind escapes me as to who did the catching. It may have been the coach, he may have brought a catcher with him or he may have had Chase catch me. When we were all done, it only lasted an hour; he shook both of our hands and told us the motto of the baseball team at the school. The motto was that God was first on everyone's list then came school and then lastly was baseball. I didn't have to look at Chase to know we were thinking our priorities at that time in our lives were very different.

He told us he was ready to make us our offers. Usually a coach will call you later or write you a letter or email. But this guy was ready to tell us face to face how much money he was going to offer us. He looked at me and said that he could give me $6,000 and then he turned to Chase and told him he could give him $7,000. I couldn't believe it, Chase wasn't even supposed to go to the tryout. This was all my idea and the guy offered Chase more. We laughed the whole way home because we knew we weren't going to go there. Neither one of us knew where we were going to go to school the next semester but we didn't care at that moment we were still too worried about having fun.

After my recruitment trip to Bethany College I was really only left with three real options. Option number one was to go to William Penn where a couple of teammates from my first season, Josh Elizando and Chris Eilers, attended. They came back over the summer and told us all about their adventures out there. The school was located in Iowa. They both complained about how cold it was and that there was nothing to do. They told us about how the talent level was not as good and that our AVC team could have beaten them. Option number two was to go to Dana College in Nebraska, I had spoken with the coach on the phone and he had sent me a package of school info. The third and last option was to give up baseball all together and attend CSUN. This last option was a scary one for me because it meant that I would have to give up the one thing that I loved so much in my life.

After looking over the material from both schools I decided that whichever school gave me the most money is the one that I would decide on. Over the next few weeks I exchanged phone conversations, emails and letters to both coaches. I sensed that I was receiving a better outlook from Coach Gorman at Dana but since I had a couple of buddies who were already attending the other school it was still in the race.

One day I received a phone call from Coach Gorman who asked me if I wanted to come out to check out the school, I accepted the invitation. I have always seen in the movies and on TV that when someone is being recruited they are always treated like royalty. I guess that was only if you were good, because I didn't get any of that treatment. I had to pay for my own flight out to the school but when I got there I could stay with some guys on the team.

So I packed my bags and I was off to the airport where I would catch a flight to Omaha, Nebraska. As I sat on the plane I kept thinking about the pros and cons of the whole situation. I would be able to continue playing baseball while the school would at least pick up some of the money for me to go to school. I would have a fresh start in a fresh place, which kind of scared me. Then I got to thinking about the cons, I would be half way across the country from my family and I wouldn't get to see them except a couple of times a year. I had a million things going through my mind on that plane ride. Eventually I came to the conclusion that I would be open minded about the trip and when I returned I could sit down and figure out what was going to be the course of action.

As we entered the town I was astonished at the fact that the town was so small, there weren't that many cars on the road and there were only a handful of stop lights throughout the town. The town of Blair only had 7,500 occupants and one main street which ran the length of the town that was made from bricks. There were only a couple of gas stations, a bunch of mom and pop owned stores and the houses were straight out of a movie. There were some fast food places but only a few sit down restaurants, definitely not any mainstream sit downs, one of which was a sports grill named Jake's. This is where Coach Gorman took me for dinner that night and we talked a little more about how my team was run and what I was looking for in a school.

The next day I headed up to the school for a tour that Coach Gorman set up for me. I was taken over to one of the academic counselor's office. This is where I would meet the biggest help to me in a period of uncertainty, her name was Denise Work and she showed me that Dana was the place for me. I went on my tour and I couldn't believe how small everything was and that the vast majority of the students lived in the dorms on campus.

Once I was seated on the plane I remember thinking that I had had a wonderful trip and this would be somewhere that I would want to go to school and play baseball. I couldn't wait to arrive home so I could tell my family all about my trip. At the time I was so excited to have this opportunity present itself. Now all I can say is this was a blessing from God that was one of many to come. God was not giving up on me he was preparing me for my rebirth.

When I arrived home I was so relieved that I found a school that I wanted to attend. I was offered a full scholarship for the $22,000 a year private school. The best part about my scholarship was that I would continue to receive it until I finished school, even though my baseball playing days would be over. I didn't know how my parents were going to take the news that I wanted to move and go to school half way across the country. They were excited that I had this opportunity but they were sad at the same time to have to let me go. They saw this as a great opportunity for me to broaden my horizons while getting a good education at the same time, it was a good deal.

I couldn't wait to tell my friends about the good news as well. When I told Tyler he was still undecided and this helped make up his mind. He wanted to attend Dana as well and spoke to the coach over the phone. He was able to land a scholarship offer and we were going to be roommates. Tyler was then able to get his friend DJ a scholarship to Dana to play third base as well. DJ then told his friend Kevin and was able to get him a scholarship to play centerfield too. I really wanted my friend Chase to come with Tyler and me but he had already received a scholarship to play to Hawaii Pacific, but he was happy for me.

3

Going Away

When I decided I was going to Nebraska to attend Dana College I needed a form filled out saying that I was of the Christian faith. At first I did not know how I was going to have this paper filled out because I did not know any pastors. My first thought was to ask Mark Winick who was a family friend and had performed my grandmother's funeral as a favor to my family. I thought he would most certainly fill out this paper and I would be on my way. But I really didn't know how to approach asking him to do this, I didn't know the guy really and I hadn't seen him since my grandmas funeral four years earlier. So I asked my mother if maybe the pastor of her church, Pastor Ken, would do this favor for me. She agreed to ask him for me.

An appointment was set up for me to meet with him. I remember he took me up into his office and sat me down for some questions. I tried to emphasize how much I wanted to go to get an education while playing baseball. I hoped this might divert some of the attention off of the religious questions that made me uncomfortable. He asked me a few questions about religion such as, if I prayed or went to church. I answered these questions as vaguely as possible because I did not want to hurt my chances of him signing the paper. After about a half an hour sit down conversation he proceeded to fill out the form and sign it.

Looking back I was given an opportunity to open my heart and have God fill my body that day, but I chose not to take the blatantly obvious signs that were right in front of me. I believe now that God wanted me to come whole heartedly to him with open arms so I could understand all He is. As Pastor Ken handed me the signed form I practically ran out the door because I had what I came for. Now there was nothing standing in my way from going to Nebraska to attend school and play ball.

While I was thinking about all of the partying, drinking and girls that were just waiting for me in Nebraska, I was neglecting the most important relationship in my life. I just didn't know it yet. I was just waiting to be unleashed into new surroundings and to experience all sorts of things that I had never done before. I think part of the reason I was so excited about all of the experiences to come stemmed from the fact that I had just begun being popular.

Another thing was the environment was just right, all of the timing just seemed right. I use "seemed right" because it was all a figment of my imagination. Without God in my life there was no direction, I just acted out of impulse. This impulse was used as a technique by the enemy to fool me into believing what I was doing was normal and okay. I now know living my life according to God's will and not my own, is how God intended for us to live. Therefore He will give us all the guidance and direction needed.

After having my parents help me move into my apartment in Blair and spending a few days with me, they left to go back home to California. This meant that I had no family and more importantly no supervision for hundreds of miles. I did not necessarily need supervision, or so I thought, but I really did. I was never a kid who would approach my parents to sit down and talk. Instead, if something was wrong I would usually wait until my mom asked me if I was alright or if something was bothering me. Now that my mother was so far away and there was no chance to come in contact with me, I was able to do whatever I wanted with no consequences. If I wanted to party into the wee hours of the night and then not go to school the next day I could, and I did.

I was surrounded by a bunch of guys who were in the same boat that I was. They moved from California and didn't know anyone in this small town that we lived in. The group of guys consisted of Tyler Bain, Dave (DJ) Medlin, Kevin Brown and me. I felt this period of my life was a time for re-inventing myself. Out of the group Tyler had only known me for two years, Dave only for about six months and Kevin I met for the first time in Nebraska. So I had the ability to start fresh in the eyes of friends, school and with life in general. I had no one to tell me what I could and couldn't do nor did I have anyone to tell me I was acting differently.

While we were unpacking all of our things in our apartment I came across a Bible that had been in my possession for a while but never read. The Bible had a green cover with the words Holy Bible stamped on the cover in gold lettering. There was an inscription on the inside cover to my mother from my grandfather. This Bible was given to me by my mother as a loaner but I never received a permanent one to be able to return the green covered one to her. I remember putting it next to my bed on my nightstand. I liked the feeling of having it there, it made me feel safe. I only read a couple of times out of it over the next few years while I was in Nebraska. It served more as a decorative piece than a functional piece.

I knew that Dana College was a Lutheran College but I was under the impression that it was on the more relaxed side. I felt nothing was being pressed upon me or forced so therefore I could afford to be naive. I would have to take a religion class in order to graduate but that was it. The prayer chapel was open every morning and anyone could attend. I never once went. Although I thought about it once or twice.

The school was small and everyone knew everyone so I saw this as an opportunity to become Mr. Cool. From day one I wanted to be someone on campus. I wanted to be the person everyone knew and everyone emulated. I wanted to be the guy that started all the trends and everyone wanted to hangout with. I wanted to be the guy who made parties the spot to be, it would only be a good party if I showed up. I knew I was a little older than most people at the school, but I saw this as a tool I could use to my advantage to manipulate people and become popular.

Before classes began all of us met with the coach up at the school. I quickly learned that Coach Gorman was only the coach because he needed a job and he loved baseball, not for any other reason. He had the opportunity and the position to help sculpt and mold young men's lives, but there was almost none of that. In fact a lot of the times the opposite was true. He broke down a lot of these kids. Most of the kids were away from home and parents, and were looking for a role model or someone they could count on. These kids wanted someone to approach when something was wrong. Coach Gorman was not that guy. He was an authoritative figure that tried to befriend the players rather than be a mentor.

Coach Gorman wanted to win and that was the bottom line. The year before the baseball team was the conference champions. Then the previous coach left and he left the team to Coach Gorman. Most of the players from the year before were seniors, so they also left. All that remained were some underclassmen backups. Coach Gorman wanted to win now and he needed a quick fix on that addiction. What he did to accomplish this was to round up a bunch of transfer students instead of bringing in freshman and rebuilding the program. If he had done it this way then he could have made the program his own just the way he wanted it. He sacrificed the program by getting transfer students who only had two seasons left to play, or in my case only one.

Gorman was not a bad coach, he did teach me lessons. I did learn while I was on that team, but everything I learned was mostly about baseball and responsibility. I could have learned so much more about life and God and how I needed to stay focused on what was important in life. If only Coach Gorman knew how important his role as a coach was to impressionable kids, he had the opportunity to be great.

As the school year began and baseball practice started I had only two things on my mind, baseball and partying. I wanted to party every single weekend, I wanted to meet new people and have fun in the process. Drinking was a huge part of my life as well as my friends. We started off drinking almost every single weekend. I would drink to escape my inhibitions. I felt if I was sober my conscience would prohibit me from having fun and not allow me to get into trouble. I used alcohol as an excuse to explore new things and test my limits.

I had only been drinking on a regular basis for about a year and my tolerance level was still not as high as my friend's. For the first few weekends I would drink so much I would become sick that night if I was lucky, the following morning if I wasn't so lucky. I felt if I drank the alcohol would allow me to experience things I had only dreamed of doing before.

For the first time in my life I felt I had a group of true friends. These guys would have my back for anything, and I would have theirs. This was our little family. We did everything together and for the most part we all got along great. We could have been called the four musketeers because wherever there was one there were all. We played ball together, we went to school together, we ate together and that was during the week. The weekends were planned by the group with the approval of Dave who we nicknamed the president of our group. I didn't have any blood family around but I did have these four guys that took the place of my family. It was unbelievable how fast all of us bonded to each other and became so close in a reasonably short period of time.

As an individual I was just an ordinary guy. But when I was around my friends or a group of people my mentality would totally change. I became so attention hungry, it was bordering on pathetic. I would look for any way to gain attention and popularity. I would accomplish this sometimes at the expense of others. During these times I would stop at nothing and let nothing get in my way of becoming who I wanted to be in my mind. This idea in my head of what I wanted to become was actually what most people would call a jerk.

If my collection of friends wanted something done they would ask me to do it and I would. I remember I was also like a test dummy when it came to things that the group was unsure of. I was pretty much open for requests and I loved all of the attention I was obtaining. If an idea was conjured up from the group I would jump at the opportunity to be the center of attention by saying or doing almost anything.

The first time it snowed while we were out in Nebraska was a good storm. It brought almost two feet of snow. This snowstorm was amazing because I had never seen the snow come down in such abundance. Growing up I can remember it snowing in my lifetime four times and it was magical every time but it didn't compare to this. There was fresh powder everywhere and it was such a bright white, it was beautiful. I don't think I was prepared for how much fun going out and playing in the snow was actually going to be.

Kevin introduced us to a new winter activity called snowskating. Snowskating is similar to snowboarding but the board is only about the size of a skateboard and your feet are not strapped in. The board is made of a hard thick plastic with grooves in the bottom. The general idea of snowskating is the same as snowboarding or skate boarding. I wasn't so much into the just cruising down a hill I wanted to do cool tricks and daring things. I think snow gave me a false sense of security in that if you fall you won't get hurt because snow is soft. The problem with that theory is that there is not always stuff you know about under the snow such as rocks or cement.

On this particular day we were all like kids in a candy store. This was by far the coolest thing we had seen since moving out to Nebraska. In California, where we came from, there is snow but you have to take a drive to the mountains to experience it. Here the snow was right outside our apartment and everywhere. All of us got dressed in our snow gear and headed out to test out our snowskates. Snowskating in the parking lot became boring after only ten minutes. Someone decided that it would be a great idea if we could snowskate off of the apartment garage roof.

Kevin drove his lifted 4 X 4 Ford F-150 truck up next to the garages and we used the truck to gain access to the roof.

After peering over the edge to find a seven foot tall mountain of snow, which was formed from clearing the apartment's parking lot, we decided this would be our landing area. Everyone was a little tentative to try it but when someone told me to go first I couldn't say no. I went for it and after the coast was clear then everyone else did it, but I was the test dummy. Needless to say I was influenced heavily on what other people thought about me and I did whatever it took to fit in.

Over the next two years I continued in my ways of sinning. I was drinking almost every weekend and by this time I was pretty good at it. I could drink hard alcohol, beer or most of the time both. I would drink just to get drunk, my goal was to reach drunkenness as fast as I possibly could and then once I got to that point I would drink to maintain that level of drunkenness.

I was bringing home all different kinds of girls for all different reasons. Some I just wanted to have fun for a night with and others I tried to start a relationship with. The ones I tried to start relationships with ended after a short while because I became bored with them. I thought that they were impeding my goal for more fun. I think a big reason I had no respect for women or for myself was because I had fallen deeper into the dirty world of pornography. I had been desensitized to reality through pornography and was relying only on fantasies that were conjured up through the viewing of pornography. This also helps explain why I became "bored" with girls, because nothing could ever live up to the fantasy in my head that I became accustomed to. Nothing was ever as good in real life as it was in my fantasies. This caused me to be in constant search to fulfill this unobtainable fantasy.

I was also engaging in some low budget crime and other menacing acts. One time we thought that it would be cool to burn down a bunch of logs that were set out for the annual bonfire the night before the bonfire was supposed to take place. We used this opportunity to make this act a fun and adventurous one. All of us dressed in all black and Dave even brought his video camera to document the experience. This was a well thought out plan and we wanted it to be the talk of the school the next day. After committing the act of starting the bonfire with some lighter fluid and lighter we hightailed it out of there. Once back at Kevin and Dave's apartment we hooked up the camera and proceeded to indulge in ourselves on the big screen. The next day at school we didn't hear one person talk about what had happened which disappointed all of us. The only mention of it was by Coach Gorman to another faculty member but it was not front page news like we had hoped and planned.

Another time we cut holes in the shapes of smiley faces in the soccer nets the night before the girls championship soccer match all because we didn't like how some of the girls treated us. This time we also made a video documentation of it and once again it garnered almost no attention.

I also continued my addiction to thievery. I stole things from stores such as my baseball glove from a sporting goods store and lots of baseball cards from a major retail chain. I also would steal things from houses that we went to for parties like watches or sunglasses. One time for Halloween we went to a house party and the group of us stole a big jar of coins from the house. After we left the party we went to Taco Bell and all of us were able to order whatever we wanted and it was all paid for by the coins.

Most of these things I did because I thought they were "cool," that they would somehow bring me respect from my peers. I would put people down because others were doing it and I wanted to fit in. My sole purpose was to be as popular as I could and I was a cut throat when it came to that. Nothing would stand in my way for my quest to be popular. I fed off of others feeding off of me, I loved attention.

One story that sticks out in my mind was around Christmas time from our first year. Our apartment complex was having a Christmas decorating contest and Tyler and I wanted to win. We both didn't have very much money and the decorations we bought were not going to be enough to win, so we came up with a plan. We went up to the dollar store at the corner and proceeded to steal Christmas decorations so that we could win the contest. This has to be one of the lowest things that we ever did.

We stole candles, stockings and even a small nativity set. We didn't win the contest.

We then came to the conclusion that what would the Christmas season be without a fresh Christmas tree in our living room. Instead of going to the tree lot and buying a tree, I went to the store and bought a drywall saw for two dollars. Then Tyler and I went looking for a tree to cut down. We went driving around town in search of a tree that would be suitable for our apartment and we found one in a park up the street from our apartment. I got out and began cutting down the five foot tree with a tiny handsaw. After about ten minutes the tree was down and we drug it to the truck and went home. All of us celebrated in our living room by decorating our new tree.

Looking back I feel so ashamed that while most people were going that extra mile to bring honor to Jesus during the Christmas season, I was destroying it. I can honestly say I didn't care about or want to believe in what Christmas was all about. I knew in my head that Christmas day was the birthday of Jesus, but that was as much thought as I had given it. I was more enthralled with giving and receiving gifts than I was with understanding the meaning of Christmas. I didn't feel anything in my heart. All Christmas was to me was a word with no feeling.

The baseball season was very fun and exciting to say the least. The best part about my entire baseball season was the fact that I was able to meet and keep many friends that I played with.

Some of the guys like Tyler Bain, Jared Bain, Dave Medlin, Kevin Brown, Justin Connors and Jarron Tate remain friends to this day. Others such as James Lal, Bobby Andrews, Greg Culver, Dustin Anthony, Mikey Smith and Matt “Fish” McWilliams were only friends while I attended school. These and others made my whole baseball experience an interesting one because they all came from different parts of the country and different backgrounds.

I enjoyed a moderate season with a 5-4 record and another average ERA. Our team was a very good team but just not a very clutch team. We had a 31-31 record and went 16-8 in our conference which allowed us to make the playoffs. Unfortunately we were eliminated and our season came to an end without any kind of a trophy. I will always look back and be able to say that this was one of the best teams and by far the best group of guys that I had ever played with.

At this point in my life I was also cursing a lot, I was around my teammates that used a ton of bad language along with the coaching staff. I didn’t have to watch out for what I might say in front of my parents because they were not around to reprimand me. I can remember when I would go home to visit my parents I would have to remind myself several times to pay close attention to what I was saying. My bad habits were pretty bad. I would catch myself mid sentence and stop before saying a curse word when I was around my parents. Overall it was just another bad habit I had become accustomed to. I thought cursing was a normal part of everyday life just like showering.

When I would go back home to visit it would always seem like a detached reality for me. I never really felt comfortable and I was never at ease because I was always worried about exposing my family to all of the negative stuff that I was doing out in Nebraska. I would have to sneak around with my tobacco and smoking. I would feel as though I was going to get caught at any moment.

Whenever I was asked about what we did or if my parents saw pictures then I would always downplay whatever I told them. I downplayed it because I didn't want them knowing all of the "bad" things I was involved in. I knew that my parents would look down on me if they knew half the stuff I was getting into. I turned into a total one-hundred and eighty degrees from how I was raised. I was also afraid that if I did get caught doing the things I was doing I would lose the funding that my parents supplied.

While spending some time at home was good I couldn't wait to get back to the lifestyle I had grown accustomed to. I would always get back to home in Nebraska and feel so relieved that I could curse, smoke, chew tobacco, drink and party without any repercussions. I loved the wild lifestyle and the spontaneity of it all. Basically I loved not growing up, not having responsibility. I wanted to be able to drop whatever I was doing and be free to do whatever I wanted. I didn't have to ask anyone whether I could go places or do things and there was no one there to tell me what time to be home. I didn't have to feel guilty about coming in late. I didn't have to worry anyone if I didn't come home for the night. My carefree lifestyle was everything I thought I wanted at the time.

Sometimes I would feel an unexplained urge, a push, to bring myself closer to God. I would experience these in very subtle ways. It was God's way of telling me I needed him in my life. He didn't come on too strong, just enough for me to pay attention. I would have something happen to me and I would think, wow what a coincidence. Then I would begin to think if it was really a coincidence or was it God. He was still preparing me for what was to come.

On a few occasions I would feel homesick or sad about something and I would gravitate to my room, if I wasn't there already, and lay on my bed. I would glance over at my dusty Bible and think about picking it up. I can remember grabbing it a couple of times and reading hoping that something profound would jump off the page and change my life. I was looking at everything all wrong. I wanted my life to change all of a sudden without doing anything. I expected to be changed without wanting to change. I didn't understand why this wasn't happening. One of the problems was I wanted God's help when things were not going well but failed to even acknowledge his existence the rest of the time.

4

Life After Baseball

After baseball season and the school year were both over I was offered a once in a lifetime opportunity. This opportunity was presented to me by Coach Gorman as a special trip for seniors from the baseball team. I was asked along with my buddy Chris Rubio. We would be representing the United States on the small island of Aruba. I didn't really know what to expect on this trip besides playing some baseball and partying. I had never been outside the United States and was a little unsure of how things were in other parts of the world.

While on the island I had many eye opening experiences. The way that this country lived in poverty was unbelievable. I was made to take a look at my own life and see how many of the everyday things I took for granted. Even though the country was poor the people were happy because their lives didn't center on material goods. The players on the ball field had ragged uniforms and equipment that was old and falling apart. It didn't matter because they loved baseball. Baseball was sort of an escape from the harsh realities of life, a private getaway for them.

As for baseball our team dominated the islanders but it didn't seem to matter to them they were just happy to have a team to play against. Our team won all five games we played and I won both games I pitched. I was able to meet some really cool guys from all parts of the United States. This experience was also special because I was able to share it with my good friend Chris Rubio. We can look back at the memories of those days and remember a once in a lifetime experience we were able to take.

I came back from this trip with many stories about how good our team did and all of the partying we did. I was overlooking the obvious. I had just seen how people were living in poverty and were trapped. I was too busy, concerned with how much fun I had playing baseball. This trip offered me experiences that I could have taken away from the island to change my perspective on life but I didn't know how to make that connection. Now I can see those changes and how God was opening my eyes to new ways of life but at the time I was unable to make the connection.

After a long summer break I was on my way back to Nebraska. I drove with Jared all the way home and arrived the Friday before school started. I was happy to be back home but I felt something missing. It didn't take long to figure out that baseball was missing from my life. It seemed as though I had just gotten back on track with my academics when I joined the AVC team and then continued with it onto Dana. Now I was facing a fresh semester without baseball and one of the worst parts was that all of my friends still had one year left of eligibility.

Trying to mentally prepare myself for life without baseball sounded easier than it really was. I would try to tell myself that I would have so much free time now to experience new things, but in reality I was just trying to psych myself out. I would go out to the practices with the guys, mainly just to feel like a part of something that was now gone. Practice was to get myself ready for the games, practice was to become better at something that will be used in the games. This is why when I went out to the field to practice with the guys I felt empty, there was no hope of me ever getting back into a game. I envied every one of those guys because they had what I ultimately wanted, a chance to get into a game. I didn't want to coach the other guys on the team I wanted to play. I didn't have any friends but the ones on the team and no one I knew was in the same boat as me. I found it very hard to understand myself and what I wanted at this time in my life, because all I wanted was to play ball and I couldn't.

I tried to help out in any way that I could at practice. I would pitch batting practice. I would help out with some of the pitchers. I would hit fly balls and even umpire some of the scrimmages. I couldn't tell if all of this was helping or hurting me to get over baseball. I would have a great week of practicing with the guys and then they would leave on a road trip. I remember feeling so alone while they guys would be away for the weekend, my only friends were on the team and without them I felt lost.

When the guys would play at home I would take pictures at the games, work the scoreboard or do some announcing just to feel like I was still a part of this team. I liked to be around the field on game days because even though I wasn't playing, it would still have the same effect on my senses. During the games I would walk into the dugout and talk to some of the players, telling them some insight that I had on the game. I would tell some players helpful hints on the other team or talk to the pitcher and find out what the hitter's are like. I would always talk to my friends through the fence and wish them good luck.

I had to endure two seasons of baseball while I was still attending Dana before I graduated. The last year was a lot easier because both Kevin and DJ were not playing as well so I would keep busy with them. We found new ways to pass the time like skateboarding in the summer and more snow skating in the winter. I also started working for the school more, by doing tours of the campus to prospective students or working the athletic games in the evenings.

I also got into more trouble without baseball in my life. I had taken a job with a company called Omaha Night Life. The company ran a website composed of pictures promoting various nightclubs and bars. The pictures were of people partying and having fun to promote the establishment. The bars and nightclubs paid the company to have photographers come out and take these pictures as advertisement for their place.

I was hired as a photographer and at the time I thought this was the best job ever. I was paid thirty dollars a night to go out and take pictures at these places. I always got in free to the bars and clubs and I would also get drinks for free. The best part was I was allowed to have an assistant. So I asked DJ. When he became my partner my job became much more enjoyable because I now had a wingman. Spending two or three nights a week in bars and clubs was not good for me at all. It made me into a person that I was not; I was feeling invincible because I thought I was a "Big Shot." This part of my life was very low because I thought that it was so fulfilling at the time but it was as empty as could be. I met many different girls during this time and used a lot of them. I thought I was so cool with this job, I would tell everyone how great it was so they could envy me.

I really had nothing at this point going for me except my education. I was experimenting with my appearance quite frequently at this stage of my life. I was experimenting with different hair styles such as long and dyed black, bleached hair and a Mohawk cut. All of my friends had tattoos but I was not to the point to deface my body with ink so I went with a little les permanent solution, piercing. I had my lip pierced and then my nose after a short while both eventually ended up coming out. I was drinking and smoking more than ever I was chewing tobacco, cussing and sleeping around. I am so thankful that I never was seriously hurt from all of the harm I put myself in. Without the presence of God in my life I had my priorities all screwed up.

Finally a shining moment came throughout all of the darkness that surrounded me. I graduated college. The day had come after nine and a half years and my family made the trip to witness it. I wrote the words FINALLY across the top of my graduation cap to express my relief. I graduated in May 2007 with a Bachelors degree in elementary education. I can still remember the smiles on my parent's faces and how proud they were of me. I felt I was now ready to start my life after all of these years in school. The only problem was I didn't want to teach. I was given a deadline from my parents that if I didn't find a job within a month, I needed to come back home. My funding was coming from my student loan checks and through my parents so I had to get going on finding a job.

Kevin found a job at a company called Continental Fire Sprinkler as an apprentice to a sprinkler fitter. Kevin helped both me and DJ get jobs as apprentices as well. While working as a sprinkler fitter I was also working towards becoming a firefighter in Omaha along with Kevin. DJ was working on becoming a police officer at this time. I had been working for this company for a few months installing fire sprinklers in different buildings when I started to become bored. I was making pretty good money and the hours were good but the repetition of the job started getting to me. I didn't like having only one person to interact with on a daily basis. I wanted to work around more people not just one guy that I didn't have anything in common with.

Outside of work Kevin moved out of our house because he and his girlfriend, at the time, were pregnant (Kevin and Lindsey are now married with two children). Now the house was filled once again with three bachelors, DJ, me and our friend from college Justin Connors. Now that we had money from working we were partying all of the time. We would go to bars or clubs every weekend. I was trying to work on my photo business by taking pictures whenever I had the chance. I would recruit girls to take pictures of and dated a few of them in the process.

In September of 2007 I traveled home for my niece Jordan's birthday. While I was home my mom was telling me how much she missed me and that she prayed for me to come home. My dad showed interest in my photography skills and was talking to me about helping me with my company if I moved back. I don't know if it was being around the family or my dad's conversation about my photography business but something got me thinking. I feel in my heart it was my mom's prayers that were heard and God started the ball rolling that day for the sequence of events that would soon come.

I arrived back home in Nebraska with an emptiness in my heart. I thought it might just be jet lag or me dreading to go back to work the next day. But when I awoke the next morning and went to work I had the same feeling. That night I called my parents and spoke to them about moving back home. Of course they wanted me home so they might have promised me a few things that weren't exactly the whole story. I was set on my decision to move back and let DJ know, he was not happy at all.

I went into work the next day and told my foreman of my decision. I told him that I would finish out the work week and I would be done. He told me that I didn't have to finish the week that I could just finish the day, I agreed. Once the decision was made to quit my job and move back to California everything happened within a day or two. My mom agreed to fly out to accompany me on the drive back to California. I packed up all of my belongings and loaded them into a U-haul trailer attached to my Chevy Blazer. When my mom arrived I was ready to get on the road and head home.

I had a farewell party with all of my friends to say my goodbyes. I was sad, but I was so excited for what lie ahead of me. My mom and I set out early the next morning headed towards California. We made it to Wyoming before my poor Chevy Blazer just couldn't go any further and gave out. We had the truck towed to a local dealer and spent the night in a hotel. The next morning we found out the truck was dead and they offered me six hundred dollars in trade. I ended up settling on a 1999 GMC Yukon Denali because I still needed something to tow the trailer. With the new truck running smoothly we made it home before we knew it. When I walked through the doorway of the house in Palmdale I was relieved to finally be back home.

It was really happening, I was moving back home to California. After three and a half years I was finally leaving the state that had offered me so much. I learned so much about myself and about life in general from my experiences in the last few years. I met so many new and interesting people from all walks of life and from all over the world. The close friends I went through so much with were now going to be half way across the country. I felt as though time had skipped me by, it had all gone so fast. It seemed like it was just the other day that I was packing up my things to move out to Blair, Nebraska and now in a blink of an eye I was on my way back to California.

The pace of Nebraska was so much slower. It allowed me to soak in much of my surroundings and perceive such a new outlook on life. I worked as a photographer and as a sprinkler fitter. I worked many odd jobs for the school such as, an announcer for sporting events, school photographer, lifeguard, on the sidelines at the football games, and as a tour guide on campus. I taught classes of students between the ages of six and thirteen, and received my Bachelor's degree in the process. I made lots of friends even some that are lifelong friends. I had played baseball for a college team and had so much fun doing so. I learned a lot about life and even more about myself.

All of this and yet something was missing in my life. God was!

I appreciated being in the moment all the time. I enjoyed the things I was doing and the way I perceived life. But I believe this was all God's plan to show me what life was really about. How empty life can be without God. I look back on my time in Nebraska now and I can appreciate all of the blessings in disguise that God gave me. I can see now my experiences were not opening my eyes to great new things, but instead they were showing me a different side of life.

I was experiencing what life was like without God as the main focus in my life. I was living my will instead of living the will God set forth for me. In a sense I was being blinded. I compare it to television, all you see is what the camera is positioned to show you, you don't see the whole picture. I felt as though I was not in the television show but instead just watching the television show. Now I can see what is all around me and I am in the television show. I know this life on earth is just a stepping stone to the awesomely beautiful afterlife in heaven that God has for us to experience. He doesn't want us to just sit around and watch the show and be intrigued by this life on earth. We need to be productive and use this life on earth to live out God's plan for us.

For a long while after I moved back home I was uncertain why I did it. I couldn't believe that I gave up everything I wanted for a flimsy hope. I tried to convince myself the reason I moved home was because I didn't want to work as a sprinkler fitter anymore. But I could only hang on the fact that life would never be the same now, I was actually trying to find ways of moving back.

I also blamed my parents for tricking me into moving back home. My dad for telling me he would help me open up my own photo studio and for my mom who made me feel guilty I lived so far away from the family. My mom kept telling me that my grandparents were getting old and my niece was growing up. I would be missing out on my family because I was off in Nebraska with a job I was unhappy with. My dad pulled the plug on my photo studio because of money. Before he made the investment he wanted me to gain more experience and start small in the area first. I don't think it was until about six months later I finally forgave both of them for my move back to California.

Once I was back at home my dad was able to get me a job at an Imaging center in Northridge. I had no idea what I was supposed to be doing nor did I have any experience in the Radiology field. The owner of the facility, Dr. Deutsch, worked closely with my dad over the years at Antelope Valley Hospital. I am not sure if my dad mislead him with my experience or if Dr. Deutsch trusted my dad to bail me out if there was any problems. Whatever the case was he gave me the job.

I was now a PACS/RIS administrator for Renaissance Imaging Center. PACS stands for Picture and Archiving Communication System and is the system for digital X-rays. RIS stands for Radiology Information System which basically manages all of the scheduling and reporting of the patients visit to radiology. My dad was and still is the PACS administrator for Antelope Valley Hospital and my brother Scott was at the time the PACS/RIS administrator for Century City Doctor's Hospital.

I figured if there were any problems I could just rely on those two to bail me out.

My first day was on October 1, 2007. It was a Monday. I was living in Palmdale at my parent’s house and decided since I was going to train all week down in Northridge I would just stay at a hotel for a couple of nights out of the week. So I packed some clothes and I left the house at six thirty in the morning to be there by eight.

Once I arrived I felt as though I had to put on a disguise for the job. The disguise was to fool everyone into believing I knew what I was doing. Behind that disguise I had no clue what I was doing. After cramming in a ton of information on the RIS system and taking pages of notes I was off to my motel room. I decided on the Motel 6 because it was only $32.99 a night. After dropping my stuff off in the room I decided to get some dinner next door at Tommy's Burger. I took my chili cheeseburger, fries and a drink upstairs to my room to eat.

After the sun went down I began to feel a little afraid since this neighborhood was not the greatest of neighborhoods. I heard police sirens, people yelling and dogs barking all through the night. I woke up the next morning grabbed my things, checked out and told myself I would rather wake up early and drive in traffic then to go through that again.

After my week's worth of training I was allowed to work from home. I used a remote access program to login to the system if there were any problems. I bragged to all of my friends that I had a really laidback job. I only had to fix problems when I was called and I would receive fifteen hundred dollars a month for my services. This allowed me to start concentrating on my photo business with all of my free time. During this time period I relied heavily on both my brother and my dad to get me out of jams.

I worked at the imaging center until March 2008. I was living at home and I wasn't doing much of anything. I wasn't going out much, I wasn't really working on my photo business and I didn't have the presence of God in my life at all. I didn't have a plan. I was just waiting for something to come to me because so many times in my life things were just given to me. Once again an opportunity was about to fall into my lap via my brother. I thought this was a great opportunity but little did I know this was the biggest opportunity of my life. God was just starting to orchestrate the unfolding of my future.

Scott had taken a job at Kaiser Permanente as a PACS administrator and told me that I would be a good candidate to fill his old position. This plan could only work because Scott was so good at his job. The director, Milton Gittens, trusted what Scott had to say and his opinion. Scott offered his recommendation to the director and the radiology manager that his younger brother fill his shoes. What a great idea, they probably thought. What better person to fill the position than someone just like Scott and with all of his knowledge.

I had the experience in the same field even though it was just a little and I could get in touch with Scott if I needed him for something. Seemed like a perfect plan. I went into the interview with my Oscar Dela Renta suit and my head held high. I was sure I already had the job. I sat down with Milton and Tom Tatum and interviewed for a position I was nowhere near qualified for and got the job.

Looking back it is so funny how Scott set everything up and I could just stroll in and get the job. Sounded so simple and I really never gave it much thought, I think that I was a little cocky and this just caused me to become more big headed. God had this whole plan laid out for me and I walked his path and tried to take the credit for it.

I went down the following week and began to train with Scott on the systems. After work he went with me to look for some apartments. We looked at a few different places. I found the one for me off of Santa Monica Blvd, a few streets away from the freeway. I signed a month to month lease for $1350 a month for a, one bedroom, four hundred and fifty square foot, built in the late fifties with no air conditioning apartment. This apartment was the first time I would be out on my own all by myself with no roommate. I was only about ten minutes away from work and ten minutes away from the beach so I was in a pretty exclusive spot. Though it was expensive to live there I could afford it because my starting salary was sixty thousand dollars a year.

5

The Meeting

I moved all of my belongings into my new apartment and even went out to get some new furniture to make it feel more like a home. I was excited to be out on my own again but it wouldn't be long for me to start feeling lonely. I only lived in the apartment during the week and would return to my parent's house on the weekends because I was lonely.

During the week I would be all alone and I didn't know anyone near by so I fell into my trap of viewing pornography even more than before. I was becoming a recluse during my

Monday thru Friday life. I would actually dread coming home from work because of the loneliness. I kept trying to convince myself I was doing well in life. But really was headed towards nothing. I was always trying to come up with plans to move back to Nebraska. I would spend my workdays looking online for jobs out in Omaha at different hospitals. I thought the solution to my problem was to go back to what I had been used to before. I felt that if I could be able to move back to Nebraska and have my friends around me then everything would be fine. The reality of the whole thing was everyone had their own lives and it would never be like when we all first moved out there and spent all of our time together.

I wasn't dating anyone and when I did finally meet someone I smothered them because I was so lonely, and she left. Every night became the same routine, I would get home from work heat up some microwavable food and then sit down and watch a movie that I had rented from Netflix. After the movie I would sit down at my computer and search the internet for filth before I took a shower and went to bed, just to do it all again the next day.

I found myself growing more and more dependent on my downward spiral of activities. I was chewing tobacco multiple times when I would come home from work and it even got to the point where I would chew in my office at work. I even took up smoking again. I would have an urge to buy a pack of cigarettes.

I would always buy menthols because I thought they didn't smell as bad. When I would get home I would stand out on my balcony and light one up. By the time I was about halfway done with the cigarette I would think how nasty it was. This charade would go on until I found myself at the counter buying another pack of cigarettes just to do the whole thing all over again.

After a couple of weeks of working at the hospital I noticed a girl working at the front desk for security. I remember I immediately thought to myself that I have to get to know her. I asked my friends at work about her and they told me that they thought she had a boyfriend, and besides I didn't have a chance with her. I reassured them I was going to make her mine.

I would have my shirts dry cleaned at work and when I would go down to pick them up I would converse with the lady that worked down there named Felicia. One day I asked Felicia about this girl in security named Johanna. Felicia told me that Johanna had a boyfriend that was a cop and that her mother, who worked as the parking manager for the building, would brag about him all the time. That day I was absolutely crushed. I set my hopes on something and now it was not going to ever happen.

A couple of days passed and I started talking to her as I passed her desk. Nothing major just "hi" or "how are you today." After the small talk we started talking about our lives outside of work. She never mentioned anything about a boyfriend. I thought to myself either she didn't really have a boyfriend, or maybe she just liked me more than her boyfriend. I would joke around with her and make fun of her hair in a cute way as an excuse to get to talk to her.

Then on Valentine's Day as I was walking down the hallway I could see some flowers on her desk and my heart sank. I wanted to just slither by her desk so she wouldn't see me but instead I acted like it didn't faze me. I walked by and said hi. In reality I was feeling as though my chance with this beautiful girl was nothing more than a dream that would never come true.

I continued to talk and flirt with Johanna when I would see her around. One day I received an email from her at work, so I started to think she actually liked me in the same way I liked her. I didn’t care how this was happening, whether she really didn’t have a boyfriend or if she had one but was thinking about leaving him, I was just glad that it was happening. I asked her for her number so I could further the conversations to outside of work. After a long day of laying cement in front of my parent’s rental house I text her to ask if she wanted to meet up that night. She agreed to meet me off of the freeway on Burbank Boulevard in a Denny’s parking lot.

Once she pulled up she told me to follow her in her car, which was a very nice looking White BMW. I don’t know what I was thinking or doing but the next thing I know I looked up and see her car stopped in front of me at a red light. I was going way too fast to slam on my brakes so I had to make evasive maneuvers. I swerved my Denali to the left and onto the wrong side of the street while totally running the red light. My heart was beating out of my chest when I pulled over a ways down the road to wait for her to catch up. I knew if I would have hit her with my truck it would have injured her and totaled her car. Thank goodness no one was coming through the signal the other way and an accident was avoided altogether.

Her car pulled up behind my truck and we agreed to leave my vehicle on the side of the road. As I climbed in her car we both looked at each other and down played what just happened with a bit of humor. We arrived at a Barnes and Noble on Ventura Boulevard and I was feeling very confident about myself in that I had actually gotten Johanna to come out on a date with me. Unfortunately I was over confident and talked about subjects that should never be brought up on a first date. I was talking about girls I had dated in the past and some other crazy times from the past. The night ended with her dropping me back off at my truck and we went our separate ways.

The next time we went out was a few days later when I invited her out to the driving range with me after work. I met her at the golf course and greeted her with some flowers that I had picked up from a Farmer's Market on my lunch break. This is the moment when Johanna tells me that she knew I liked her. I had just gotten my new driver about a week earlier and was having fun absolutely crushing the ball when Johanna asked if she could use it. I allowed her to use it but explained to her that it was new and expensive. We had fun and decided to see each other that weekend.

For our next date we went to Universal City Walk and went to a sports bar. We played some pool, had a couple of drinks and then walked around looking in different shops. I was really beginning to like Johanna, she was fun to be around and smart with a good sense of humor. Every time I was with her I was enjoying myself immensely and couldn't help but to have a gigantic smile. When the date was over I would be thinking about her all the time and would wonder if she would do the same.

I would spend a lot of my work day texting, emailing or talking with Johanna. My days were centered on her. I remember one day she let me take her to a place down the street to get lunch. We walked down to this restaurant and sat down and ate together. On the way back we were about a block away from our work and I leaned over and kissed her. She was shocked that I did this in public and she was embarrassed because there was a guy from our work behind us that saw. I didn't care who saw us because that is just the way I felt for her, but apparently she wasn't quite ready for that.

After dating for a month I felt I knew enough about her and liked all of it that I wanted to ask her to be my girlfriend. I went out and bought a greeting card and wrote in it how I felt about her. At the bottom of the card I wrote I just had one question "Would you be my girlfriend?" On August 21st I gave her the card and I waited anxiously while she read it. She blushed and told me of course she would with a big smile, we hugged and kissed. I remember at that moment I felt like I was floating on air.

We already had a date set up to go to the Long Beach Aquarium so we left. Before the aquarium we had lunch, after only spending about two hours at the aquarium we left. We didn't want to go back home so we went to a bar and had a couple of drinks. This was on a Sunday so we didn't stay out too late but we had a wonderful day and when I arrived back home I was just about jumping with joy. I would need all the joy in my life I could get because we were unsure about what was going to happen the next day at the hospital. When we left the previous Friday we heard rumors of the hospital closing its doors.

I woke up and got ready for work just like every other day. Even though I was unsure if the hospital would still be open when I arrived. I remember feeling if the hospital was going to go bankrupt then I was prepared for it and would be just fine. When I got to work people were standing outside and they were not letting the employees in the building. I met up with a couple of coworkers outside and couldn't believe what was happening. I was not prepared for the feeling of helplessness I felt. I called

Johanna to meet up with her to try and figure out what was going on and what was going to happen.

I kept thinking I didn't want to work anywhere else without Johanna because I had become so accustomed to seeing her everyday. If I was forced to move I felt our relationship would be totally different and may not weather the storm. All I had were negative thoughts about our relationship crumbling and then I would be all alone again.

I found Johanna in the operator's office which was merely an old patient room made into an office. Some of the hospital floors were totally vacant and they were used for offices. My office for instance was an old patient room. It was nice because I had my own bathroom, with a shower, and it had very large windows. I told her I needed to speak with her and she stepped out of the office and left the other operator to field the calls.

We went to the empty patient room next door and began to talk about what was going to happen with the hospital. We both had our different ideas of what we thought was going to happen. One thought was maybe the hospital would be purchased by another medical facility and then we would remain in our current positions. But we both had to brace ourselves for the fact that we would be without jobs. Without a job would cause me to have to move and it would cause Johanna to have to give up her prized possession, her BMW. Before I left I gave her a hug and a kiss, it would be the last time I ever kissed her at that hospital.

I was allowed to pack up all of my belongings and then leave the premises. The hospital closed due to bankruptcy on Monday August 22, 2008, one day after I had asked Johanna to be my girlfriend. I was optimistic in the hope of retaining my job, but I had to be realistic too. I put in a thirty day notice to my apartment manager later that day. I was hoping I would receive my last paycheck from the hospital, but it never came and they ended up robbing me for right around three thousand dollars. Johanna was allowed to stay on to help out with the security for the hospital and stayed about two weeks longer.

Unfortunately I had to move back into my room as a kid growing up and stay with my parents. I was thankful they allowed me back in with open arms. I was also thankful my parents allowed me to get my feet back on the ground with no income. My relationship with Johanna was hard because of all of the driving involved. We were growing closer even though we were farther apart physically. We spent a lot of time on the phone finding out about each other. Anytime I had the chance I would drive down and visit her.

I began looking for a job almost immediately. It was hard because of my experience level and the fact that I had only spent five months at the hospital and another four months at the imaging center. I tried to file for unemployment benefits but I was unable to qualify, which would later turn out to be such a blessing. I did land a contracted job with the hospital setting up a retrieval system for patient data. This only lasted a total of four days but did pay me one thousand dollars.

Finally I found work through my old manager at the imaging center, Carmen Cooper, where I had worked. She was also the radiology manager for the outpatient clinic for Antelope Valley Hospital and knew my dad well. She told me she had a position as a delivery driver for the local area delivering x-ray films. The job was far from what I was making before, I would only be making nine dollars an hour, but at least I would have some income. Although I was thankful that I was able to land a job that would hold me over in the meantime I couldn't help but think this job was nothing more than short period solution until something better came along. I knew this job was not going to be a career so I every chance I got I was looking for another job to get me back out on my own towards a better future.

Since returning back home I had accompanied my mom a couple of times to church, but still didn't feel as though my life was in order to be there. I went a couple of times to church with Johanna and her family as well. We went to a Christmas Special and another time for New Years. I felt disconnected every time I went to church because I knew my heart was not pure and that I didn't belong there.

6

The Event

One day I had an argument with Johanna and the situation got really ugly. She wrote me an email, called and told me to read it. I was working when she told me about the email. I was on my rounds in Palmdale so I decided to stop by home and read it. When I opened up the email I about fell out of my chair, it was a breakup email. It felt like my heart had been ripped out of my chest and slammed on the ground and then jumped on. I was sad, upset and angry all at the same time.

I didn't understand, I thought we had gotten through the worst of things and we were heading in the right direction. I tried to talk about things but it was too much to talk about over the phone. I was crying and she was crying and we both were yelling at each other. Finally we hung up with her not wanting to be with me anymore. We didn't talk for the rest of that day or the following day as well.

In the meantime I was trying to come up with a plan that didn't make any sense at all. I was going to try and win her back by raising money and then secretly sending the money to her. The money was for her to go to college to become a nurse. I wanted to start off by giving her around three thousand dollars. I figured the only way that I could come up with that type of money fast was to sell my most expensive and prized baseball cards. I went and retrieved my cards, scanned them into the computer and wrote descriptions for all of them to be placed up for sale on EBay.

The first ones to go in my collection were the seven 1909 T-206 cigarette cards. This group included a Christy Mathewson, Cy Young, Frank Chance, Hal Chase, Rube Marquard, Jap Barbeau and a Patsy Dougherty. These cards had all been graded by a third party grading company named PSA. This in turn increased there value and made them more of small investments rather than collectibles. These cards had been purchased about eight years earlier and were the cornerstone of my graded card collection, they would have been a nice addition to any collection.

After not talking to Johanna the next day I started thinking my time was slipping by to get her back. I didn't want to, or better yet couldn't accept the fact that she was leaving me. I understood in my heart we were meant for each other and we already went through all of the stress of being apart. But I was terrible at showing her how I felt, usually when it mattered most.

Instead of driving down and talking with her and patching things up I decided I was not going to let her know how much she hurt me. I went around my room and packed up all of the pictures, letters, gifts and anything else that reminded me of her and put them all in a big box. I took the box and loaded it into my car and began driving down to her house. When I arrived at her house it was probably around nine at night, I parked down a side street and unloaded the box. I walked across the street and delivered the box on her doorstep and then proceeded to send her a text message telling her about the box on her porch.

I waited across the street until she came out and looked in the box. She immediately called me and started yelling and crying about what I had done. All she was waiting for me to do was comfort her and tell her that everything was going to be okay. Instead I just made matters worse by doing the complete opposite by throwing in the towel. I called her and stayed talking to her on the phone about how all I really wanted was to be happy with her and make her happy. After about half an hour on the phone we decided to meet.

When she came out of the house and got into my car we hugged. I told her I didn't want her ever to leave me and that everything would be okay. I knew part of the reason that we were struggling was the fact I didn't have a relationship with God to be able to draw strength from in times of need. I understand now looking back how important a relationship to God is in a relationship and how much it affects both people involved. It also takes a great deal of stress away from problems that arise in relationships because if you are close in faith to the Lord, He will keep your thoughts positive. He will also allow you to give your problems and worries to Him and in turn he will comfort you and provide answers and solutions.

Once Johanna found out about me putting up those baseball cards to sell on EBay she told me to stop selling them. I was feeling a little depressed about my income level and wanted to make more money so I left them to sell. That weekend I remember sitting on the couch at Johanna's house watching my auctions end on EBay. That first group of seven cards generated around three thousand five-hundred dollars. Both Johanna and my eyes lit up and I became money hungry at that point. I had always known that my baseball cards were worth money but now that they had sold I was really excited about selling all of these little pieces of cardboard.

I couldn't put my baseball cards up fast enough on EBay. I started off putting up all of my graded cards which were my high investment cards. After those were gone I started selling anything I could find that would bring me in good money. At the same time I decided to sell my eighty four shares of Microsoft stock and my thirty three shares of Time Warner stock. I took a huge hit on both of these. The market was bad and I only sold them for a quarter of the six thousand dollars that I paid for them. I told Johanna I was saving all of this money for when we were to get married, but at that point she didn't really believe me.

I found out I could be approved for unemployment benefits after three months. This approval led me to quit my job in January 2009, with no prospective jobs in sight. The main reason for this move in my life was so I could spend my time looking for a job while I was receiving income. I was making the maximum amount, which was nine hundred and fifty dollars every two weeks. I was looking for a job and didn't really want to find a quick fix job I wanted to find a career that I could stay with permanently.

In the meantime I was working side jobs for Johanna's parents remodeling their house. I started off remodeling the kitchen. I was granted permission from Johanna's parents to stay the night on a mattress in the living room floor for the time that I was working there. I began work by removing all of the kitchen doors and drawers for the cabinets and sanded and stained all of them along with the cabinets. After my work was complete on the cabinets I spoke with her parents and we decided on a complete remodel of the kitchen. The remodel involved replacing the floor, painting the walls and replacing countertops and sink.

I started demolition work on the kitchen by ripping up the floor. I took up the linoleum only to find another layer of linoleum and then under that was another layer. After getting down to the wood floor I began working on the countertops. I took all of the tile off of the countertops which turned out to be quite a job because of the inch worth of cement that was holding the tiles in place. The timeframe I promised was not going to happen. It was taking longer than I originally planned but things were going fairly smoothly.

About halfway through the kitchen project is when my life took a drastic turn. My life changed from that moment on. I remember it was raining that night and I was just winding down for the night when Johanna approached me. She had a look on her face that I will never forget. She was holding my laptop in her hands and asked me "what is this!" The tone in her voice was upset. She wanted to hear an answer she knew but didn't understand. My laptop was turned to show me a pornographic website. I knew right away I wanted to get away from this problem. I had been caught with my hand in the cookie jar.

I tried to down play the situation and reassure her it was not a big deal, but inside this problem was a huge problem. This was a problem that had been festering inside me for a long time. A long long time. I had grown up with this problem and it had progressively gotten worse. It had gotten worse over time because no one had ever exposed my secret before. This secret was so big and I had held it in for so long that it grew into an addictive monster. I used this disgusting habit to seek comfort. The moment I was exposed by Johanna was the moment I became the outsider looking in. I saw a glimpse of how disgusting it was and how big of a problem it really was. I also saw the pain that I had caused in the eyes of my girlfriend and wanted to just make it all go away.

I burst out the door and began walking, with no jacket on, in the pouring rain. I had no destination I just wanted to get away. I needed time to figure out what I was going to do. While getting soaked in the rain I had the most confusion in my mind; it was almost like a civil war within my brain. Part of me wanted to give up on our relationship while the other part wanted to go and work things out. Then I was torn between lying about the whole thing and trying to wiggle my way out of it and coming clean with the entire truth. At the moment when I knew that she hated me the most Johanna called me and told me to get back to the house. I tried to argue with her that I should just leave and why did I need to go back, but she stayed strong and demanded that I come back to the house.

I walked back to the house and arrived at the side door to the kitchen where Johanna stood in the doorway with a towel to let me back in. I came in and sat on the couch and began pouring out my heart. I figured if she knew most of the problem already then this was my opportunity to expose the whole beast of a problem. To get it all out into the open, because I desperately needed help. The moment was tough to get through and I really wanted to just give up because I felt I was trapped. I had kept this secret inside that was ruining my life. I was secretly living a double life.

I sat on the couch feeling so little. I was this guy who really had it all and now I felt I was a nobody because I had been exposed. I began to open my heart up and let everything pour out. I talked about how I had started this downward spiral in about eighth grade. It had progressively gotten worse over time with my fantasies crossing over to the real world. What I mean is I crossed the line of using people I came in contact with, people I worked with or went to school with, combined with all of the websites, pictures, videos and magazines to create my fantasies. I began mixing fantasy with reality and it was such a disgusting downward spiral because it became a hunger I could never feed or fulfill.

Johanna sat next to me and took everything in and she stayed strong, she took my hands and prayed with and for me. This was the first time we ever prayed together and through all of the tears and darkness this was a very special moment I will never forget. I felt so relieved inside to get all of that negative stuff out, but I was far from out of the woods from the problem. I knew I had hurt Johanna deeply, I didn't know exactly how deep but I would later find out. She showed an amazing amount of courage by staying by my side, reassuring me that everything would be just fine. I am so thankful the Lord gave her the strength to sit through and endure what she had to go through. I knew from that moment I would spend the rest of my life making things right if I had too. I was willing to do whatever it took even if I had to go to the edge of the universe and back for her I was committed to doing so.

7

Being Saved

I went through many changes throughout the next few weeks but none was more important in my life than that night with Johanna. She opened up her heart and vowed to help me rid this problem from my life. Exposing my problem to her was the hardest thing I have ever done in my life, afterwards the change was easy. Like the Bible says "The truth shall set you free" and it did.

After we both cried our eyes out, the truth started to settle in about all of the parameters of what it was going to take to try to restore things. It wasn't until the next night in my bedroom that I was saved. I remember the feeling of a huge weight lifted off of my chest when I opened my heart and received Jesus Christ as my Lord and savior. I asked for forgiveness, mercy and above all thanks for the chance I was being given. That night was the greatest night of my life, which was the night my life would be forever changed. I was released from my bondage that I was being held captive in and the feeling is something I cannot explain. It was beyond liberating. I can actually remember the feeling of being able to breathe easier and almost as though I had a weightless feeling inside. All of the evil built up inside was taken away that night and I am forever grateful for that.

I began taking steps for help. I went to a Christian website about how to combat sexual addiction and pornography and how to become pure again. There were many useful tools on how to rid my life of all filth and live my life according to how God intended. I didn't want to attend any therapy sessions or any centers for help instead I wanted to further my relationship with God. I was surprised to learn how many men suffer from the same addiction I had. I learned that people from all walks of life suffered and even pastor's had been afflicted. I drew strength from other people's testimonies and started looking at the positives instead of dwelling on the negatives. I stopped thinking about how long I suffered instead I was thankful it had not persisted one day longer and I had the rest of my life to live in the light of God.

I firmly believe if I put my life in the hands of a ten step program I would fail, but if I put my life in the hands of God I would never fail. If I relied upon man made techniques as opposed to the word of God then I would fail. I had nothing to lose if I failed in a program because I could find a variety of excuses. But if I became a man of God and placed my life in His hands then I would have everything to lose. Therefore the choice was obvious for me. I wanted to live my life for God and put my life and salvation on the line. This was a bet I wasn't going to make unless I was positive I wanted to change. In a couple of short days I was feeling better than ever because God was filling me spiritually. I knew I wanted to feel like this forever and never wanted to return to the life I had before.

I went the next day to church to speak with the pastor. I asked the receptionist to speak with the pastor. She told me the pastor was not in and asked if I would like to speak with the youth pastor. I agreed and she called him up to meet me. When he arrived I shook his hand and he showed me back to his office where we could speak privately. I barely let him take his seat before I started blurting out the reason why I had come. I openly confessed to all of the problems I was having and I seriously wanted to build on my relationship with Christ.

God placed this pastor in this very circumstance to help guide me down the right path. He listened to all I had to say and once I was done explaining my situation he began to tell me that he was glad I had come in and that I was on the right path to correct this problem. He told me that pornography was a big problem but it would be a fixable problem as long as I was willing to work hard and how to draw strength from God. He showed me how to overcome this by showing me how it destroys relationships and one of the best ways to help overcome it was to have an accountability partner. He told me by surrounding myself with people of God and by becoming involved in the church this would help build my relationship with God. He invited me to a men's breakfast that Saturday at the church. He told me the guys would be a little older than I was but they would help provide some insight.

After my discussion with the pastor he helped me understand that with the power of Christ in our lives we can overcome anything. He invited me to become more involved in the church and told me about a program called "The Truth Project." I left the church that day filled with the Holy Spirit, I was on a mission to live my life for Christ. I kept building upon all of the positive feelings I was having.

After I left I couldn't wait to call Johanna and tell her all about what I just went through. She tried to sound enthusiastic but it was so hard because I had deeply hurt her and severely damaged our relationship. I was hurting inside because I was feeling so positive and Johanna was almost feeling the exact opposite. I went home and downloaded a free program that was installed on my computer that would send a message to her email if I was looking at anything that I was not supposed to.

Another problem was that I had things from past relationships that were still in my possession and I didn't even know why. I started going through all of my belongings and throwing away anything from past relationships. I had lots of stuff that I should never have brought into my relationship with Johanna. Now all they were doing were pouring salt into an open wound. I had pictures, letters, and gifts from past relationships. I threw them all in the trash. Most of all I didn't have a good reason why I still had them but I knew I had no need for them and got rid of everything.

It was hard to pretty much start all over again in the middle of our relationship. This caused a lot of trust issues. I had to work on trying to help Johanna understand my rebirth which meant there would be no returning to my past. I would not do the same things I had done to her in the past. This was hard for her to believe and trust me due to all of the stuff I had put her through. This was a double edged sword and I knew and kept telling her if we just can get through this then everything would be fine. The saying "Time heals all wounds" kept coming up in my mind but in our case it was not happening soon enough.

I felt and still feel terrible that one of the most exciting times in my life, becoming a man of faith, was surrounded by negativity and could not be fully enjoyed because of all of the pain I caused Johanna. These times were very hard to endure because of all of the dishonesty present before. The situation had been compounded because Johanna's ex-boyfriend had proven to be dishonest and cheated on her. She felt I had come into her life and would do nothing to compromise her trust because I truly loved her. Well it turned out I did a whole lot in the area of dishonesty and the healing process was going to take twice as long because of what happened to her before.

I started attending church by myself for the early service. At the first service I went to I saw the youth pastor. I asked him about "The Truth Project" and he told me the group met every Wednesday from seven to nine at night in a room on the church grounds. I told him I would like to come by and check it out; he told me it was supposed to only be for people under twenty five years old, but I could attend. I had no prior knowledge about what this program was all about but it appealed to me and I knew I wanted to be involved with it.

My first Wednesday night I attended "The Truth Project" I was a little nervous. I didn't really know what to expect, it kind of brought me back to the nights in my uncle's room. I didn't want to feel put down because of how little I really knew. At the time this was a real fear of mine even though now I know that I should never have felt that way. I was excited to learn and wanted to soak up all of the information I could.

The Wednesday night's involved an hour watching a twelve part DVD series in which Dr. Hackett shows how to look at life with a biblical view. While watching the videos, notes were being taken on the handouts that were hgiven out at the beginning of the session. Then for another hour we sat around and discussed what went on in the video and if there were any questions to be answered.

I sat down and met the small group of four other "students" and the "teacher" along with the youth pastor who I already knew. We began watching the video, right away I was intrigued by how the host of the show was so captivating. He grabbed my attention within the first five minutes and before I knew it the lesson was over and I was left wanting more. I took notes throughout the lessons and when we had the discussion I only offered my opinion or my outlook when I was asked.

As soon as I left the church I called Johanna about how amazing this experience was. I shared with her what I had learned from the lesson and then I learned from the discussion. We were still struggling to find some peace in our relationship at this time. She was always questioning me and never believing anything I told her, which was perfectly normal. I on the other hand had to continue down the right path and continue building upon what small trust I was given.

I tried every possible way to help her see what I was seeing. I would compare my life before Christ like wearing a blindfold and now the blindfold was taken off so I could see all of the glories of God. It was hard to convey these thoughts to her, because she was always second guessing what I told her. I wanted her to be able to spend a day in my body to see and feel what I was going through. For her to be able to feel how sorry I was for the hurt I caused her and for her to feel the incredible amount of love I felt towards her.

I wanted to correct the wrong I did and to reassure her I would never go back to the past. I tried to convey this theory through asking her if she would ever go back to her ex-boyfriend, and of course the answer was no. I told her the feeling was the same for me. I was so disgusted and repulsed by my past actions that I would never go back to them. Also now I could see the most beautiful person in the world standing in front of me. I would have no reason to backtrack only to keep moving forward with the best thing in my life.

I kept on working hard towards my goals and never stopped. Now that I could see the light I didn't want to ever step outside of God's light. After receiving blessings from Him I never wanted to be without Him in my life again. I continued to go to the Wednesday night lessons and even though the class size dwindled down to just myself and the instructor, I always enjoyed the experience. I finished the program after twelve weeks and I couldn't stop talking about how much of an impact the lessons had on my life. I would tell people about them and how great they were, my grandma especially enjoyed when I talked about them.

One day Johanna called me and told me she was not feeling well. So I told her that I would come down and take care of her. She was still not letting down her guard and told me not to come down. I of course didn't listen and left my house at six in the morning. When I arrived she was a little surprised, and I think deep down inside she was excited. I took her sister Michelle to school for her and then came back to be with her. I let her sleep and I made her tea and soup trying to be there for her as much as possible. We watched a movie together and enjoyed each other's company.

I did a couple of things around the house like cleaning debris off of the roof from the neighbor's trees and even did the dirty dishes. In the afternoon I picked up Michelle from school and returned back home to take care of the love of my life. I think this was the first time since my problems were exposed she saw I was truly and deeply sorry and I would never let it happen again. She was starting to see I would be the man she always wanted me to be.

I continued to look for a job while I was receiving my unemployment benefits. I applied for jobs almost everyday, a wide assortment of jobs. I applied for computer, teaching and healthcare jobs. I was having little luck because of the poor economy. I did get a chance to take a test for the school district for a computer technician job but did not pass the test. I thought the questions being asked were far beyond what an elementary school computer technician should know. I felt if you could pass the test then you probably wouldn't be looking for a fifteen dollar an hour job.

I also saw a job as a child development teacher's assistant. I felt I was actually over qualified, but I was desperate for work. I went in to apply for the job and the woman told me I needed to have my child development certificate. This required a semesters worth of classes at the junior college. I told her I had my bachelor's degree, thinking this would override that single semester of classes. She said they still required the certificate, which didn't make any sense to me. I had a couple of other leads but nothing too serious at the time.

I was still doing home improvement jobs for Johanna's parents and through this opportunity I was enjoying the time I was able to spend with her. I finished up the kitchen which looked amazing and a hundred times better than before. I laid Spanish tile on the floor where the linoleum used to be. I put in a solid one piece granite countertop and installed a stainless steel sink. The room had been painted a nice pastel green and I added a tile backsplash along with a granite tiled countertop on a cabinet next to the refrigerator. Her parents bought a stainless steel refrigerator to top off the new look and it looked spectacular. Even though I was unable to find work I was following God's word by staying productive with these jobs.

Valentine's Day was quickly approaching and I wanted to show Johanna how much I really cared for and loved her. I wanted to make this a special night for her because I know how much pain I had caused her only a few weeks earlier. I took Johanna's younger sister, Michelle, with me to Macy's to get her a pretty dress and some shoes. I picked out a black dress I knew would look ravishing on her and then some black patent leather Guess shoes.

I felt in my heart it was going to take above and beyond the regular call of duty, to try to fix things. I didn't expect things to change over night but I did want to do more for her than the usual to plant the seed that I really did think the world of her. We went to a nice restaurant and had a lovely dinner; it was a beautiful evening and a step in the right direction.

Soon after Valentine's Day Johanna received a job from a senior assisted living facility as a property manager. The job seemed like a sweet deal, she would be making ten dollars an hour and they would supply her with a two bedroom apartment with all of the utilities paid for. The apartments were beautiful they were spacious with high ceilings and granite countertops. The best part was the apartments were brand new with no previous tenants.

Johanna started work and was promised the apartment upon completion of construction, which was in a month. I was glad she had gotten the job but I was used to having her around all day and now she wouldn't be. She was so excited for the opportunity to be able to move out on her own. We both talked about living together when we got married but I think at that point in our relationship it was just talk. I wanted more than anything to marry her and live happily ever after, but I felt she wasn't quite there yet. I still needed to prove to her a little more of my intentions and show that I was capable of keeping up my end of the bargain. I continued to pray for God to take care of us and help repair and strengthen our relationship. I also prayed for a job so I could start to make things happen in our relationship. I would always tell Johanna we could get married once I received a job and could support us.

Even though I was out of work I was using my handyman skills to get by that I learned from my dad and through experience working for him. After the kitchen was complete I started work on the living room. I ran a chair rail around the room which divided it nicely to paint the lower section a darker brown and be able to paint the upper section a yellowish brown. I also put up crown molding around the entire room to add a nice finishing touch. I used a different type of molding to construct a six foot by five foot rectangle on the ceiling that allowed me to paint inside of the rectangle the darker brown. Both of her parents, Reyes and Maria, were ecstatic with all of the work I had done. Johanna would agree with her parents and let me know how talented and artistic I was in my construction.

At this point in our relationship we were getting back to a stable position. We made the decision to purchase cell phones together. It might sound funny but this was a big step in our relationship at the time. We were being asked to sign a contract longer than we had known each other. We ended up getting our Verizon phones and called it our first major purchase as a couple. It was the small everyday things that helped get our relationship back on track, little baby steps. I had to learn to be extremely patient and not expect change to come in huge strides or very quickly.

Here I am with my mother's dad, my grandpa who was a Brown and Bigelow salesman, an artist and a Gideon amongst other things.

In this picture I am with my dad's parents, who moved from Nebraska to Van Nuys, California.

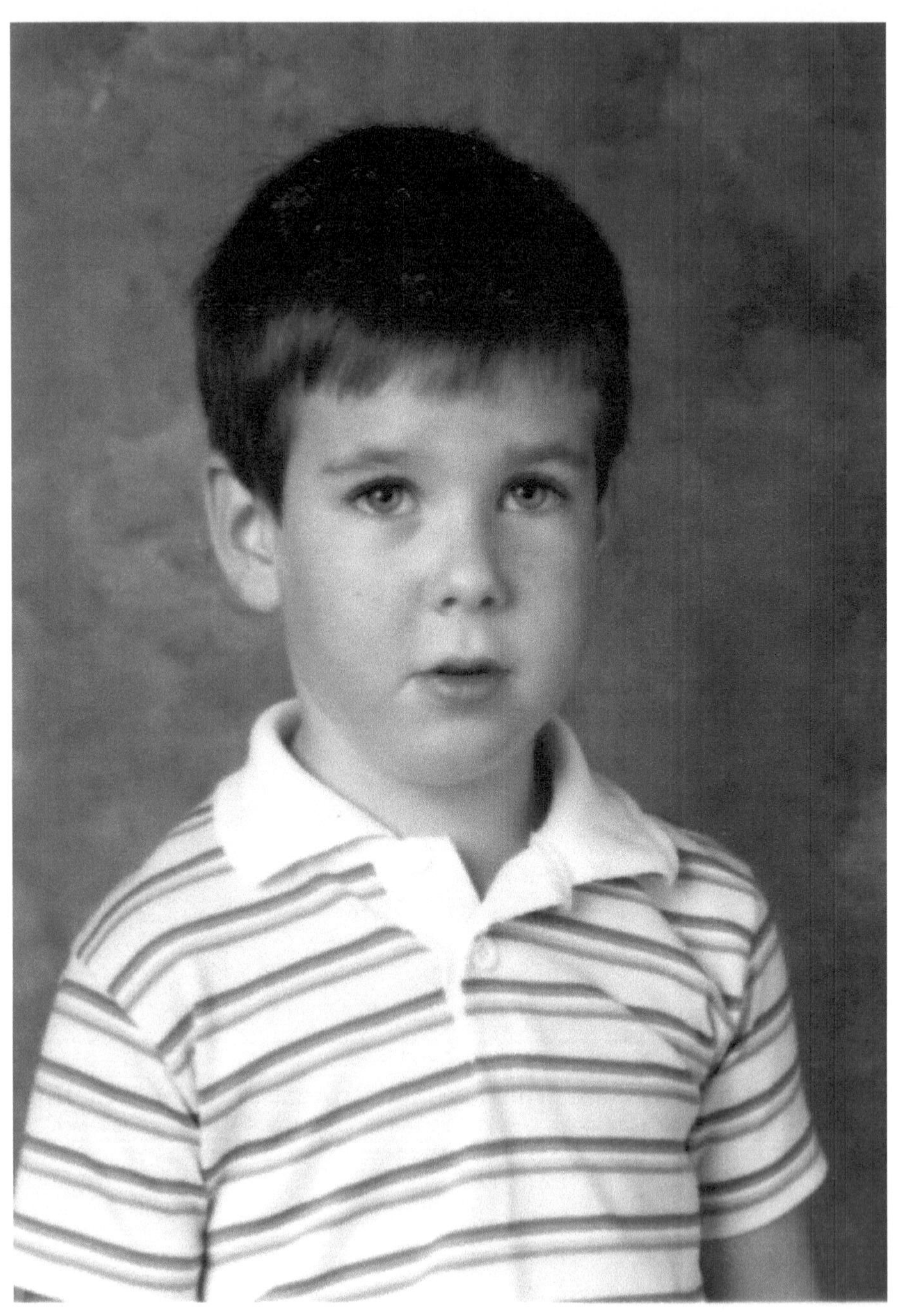

Here is a school picture from when I was in kindergarten.

This family picture was taken in 1990.

Here I am with my brother, Scott, and my sister, Melissa having fun making ice cream in the kitchen.

Here is a family picture of the entire family. From left to right, upper: my dad, my mom, Aunt Yoli, Uncle David, Grandma Mert, Grandpa Merritt. Middle Row: Grandma Gen, my brother, cousin Matt, Uncle Roger. Bottom Row: Me, my sister, cousin Erica, cousin Mark.

I always loved the Christmas season as a child.

Here is a picture of me and my grandparents at their house in 2004.

Here I am with Chris Rubio in Aruba in the summer of 2005.

Left to right: DJ, Me, Tyler and Kevin. My first and last season at Dana College.

Here is a picture from 2006, a period of time when I was trying to experiment with my look.

Here I am at a bar in Lincoln, Nebraska, about a month after moving to Nebraska, with my friends. Tyler (left), Kevin (middle) and DJ (right).

We are on a cruise to Mexico in 2009, about a month before I asked Johanna to marry me.

This is a picture from Valentine's Day 2008.

Here I am with Chase at his wedding.

This picture of me holding my niece Jordan was taken on our Mexican cruise.

A wedding picture with my beautiful wife.

8

The Decision

During my time spent at Johanna's parent's house I was growing closer and closer to her. Although I still felt her guard was up because she was still filtering everything I did. While I was finishing up the living room I decided one day to go look at an engagement ring for her. I had no intentions of buying a ring, just to look at prices and see what I would have to save to buy her the ring I wanted for her. I went to Robbins Brothers in Woodland Hills. I left the house when Johanna went to work so I had some time, but I did have to pick her sister up from school at two o'clock.

When I entered the store I started looking around and checking prices and deciding what would be the perfect ring for her. There were so many different things to take in I was overwhelmed at first. I had to decide what type of cut I wanted the diamond, then if I was going to get a ring with just one stone or several. The next step was to decide whether to get the band in gold, white gold or platinum. All of these decisions while keeping price in mind. I knew that I wanted to spend a good amount of money on the ring because this was a once in a lifetime event. I had visions in my mind of how I wanted her to react when she saw the ring for the first time and I wanted her to be absolutely floored. The other thing that crossed my mind was I wanted her to be able to be proud to show the ring off to everyone and anyone.

After walking around the store at least three times with an associate from the store I finally found it, the ring that would be perfect for Johanna. Between being in awe of the ring and excited that I had actually found the perfect ring I was coerced into actually thinking about buying the ring. Because of a promotion they had going at the time for no interest, no payments for a whole year the sales associate talked me into buying it. I purchased the ring on April 8th, I had really done it. They told me they would have to special order the ring and it would take about six to eight weeks to get it in. After all of the paper work was finalized I glanced at my watch and realized I had been there for almost three hours and I was late to pick up Michelle.

I left the store with a smile from ear to ear. I never realized spending that much money for something would leave me so happy. On the drive over to pick up Michelle I had a million thoughts running through my head. I was thinking about when and where I was going to propose and how I was going to do it. I didn’t know how on earth I was going to keep a secret of that magnitude for that amount of time. Then the reality of it sank in, I didn't have a job. How on earth was I going to convince Johanna's parents to let me marry their daughter when I didn't have a job?

I kept on praying I would get a job so I wouldn't have to worry about how I was going to provide for Johanna. That Friday I drove down to Pasadena to take the CBEST, a test to be able to teach in California. I was hoping to pass to be able to become a substitute teacher. I sat in front of the computer and I tried to rush myself to finish. I didn't take the time I needed to do a really good job. When I was finished with the test I still had plenty of time left to go back and make changes. I chose to leave instead. I received my test results for the five hour long test about two weeks later. I passed the math with a really high score, the reading part I also passed and the writing part I missed by one point. Another dream crushed, I felt like I was getting bites on my fishing line only to reel it in to find the fish had wiggled off.

I found the hardest part in my relationship with Johanna was to rebuild trust. I would pray for God to comfort Johanna and relieve the stress I was putting on her. She was going through times where we would have a perfect relationship one day and then hit rock bottom because of trust issues the next day. Johanna would still question me about certain things and accuse me of other things.

This was a very difficult time in our relationship because I wanted nothing else in the world but to be happy with Johanna. I loved her and I was set on marrying her and spending the rest of my life with her. This was hard because she was also making my life miserable with all of these accusations that were not true. Her mind was over thinking situations and placing doubt in what I was telling her. It really was a helpless feeling I had when she would get in those moods because I had no proof but the proof in my heart. I couldn't show her anything tangible to support my story. She had no faith in me and that was the single thing that could set me free. No matter how hard I tried I couldn't make her understand she was everything in my life and I didn't want or need anything else.

We kept praying about me finding a job, and I was still looking for pretty much anything. I was contacted about a job offer from a friend of my brother's named Barzin. He was in the middle of purchasing a computer store in Los Angeles and he was looking for someone to run it. I began talking to him and found out that he was doing a remodel on the store once the purchase went through. I was telling him about the remodeling jobs I had done for Johanna's parent's house and offered my services to him. He agreed to let me do the remodeling work. I was so excited to tell Johanna about the opportunity and the fact that our prayers were answered. I would plan to do the remodel and then work the store as a more permanent job. At this point in time this was better than nothing and it would help bring in some income.

This opportunity turned out to be a blessing in disguise. I met with Barzin and showed him pictures of the remodel jobs I had done at Johanna's parent's house. He was impressed with the work I had done and so we continued discussing costs. I walked the store with him. Johanna jotted down all of the measurements I gave her and the quick notes of what was to be done. This would be the biggest job of my handyman career, but I was ready for it. Most of the work was pretty straight forward and easy, or so I thought at the time.

The "to do list" entailed a long list of jobs ranging from demolition work to carpentry work. He wanted the ripping up of the existing carpet and laying laminate flooring to give the appearance of a hardwood floor. The counter was going to be resurfaced with a brand new laminate and a couple of extra shelves would be added. An adjoining wall connecting two offices was to have a doorway put in. Ceiling tiles would be replaced, painting would be done, a chair rail would be installed and the outside sign would be painted.

I priced out all of the materials and the time that I would be putting in and submitted my quote, I would stand to make around two thousand dollars. This came at a perfect time. I thought I could use the money to put towards the wedding. I was thinking through my prayers everything was going to be solved. It is funny how God uses experiences to show all his power and glory, I never saw this blessing until after the whole experience was over.

I was still waiting on Barzin to finalize the deal to obtain the place. In the meantime I was scheduled to attend a seminar on "The Truth Project." This seminar was to be able to obtain the twelve DVD's, all of the study materials with them and the approach on conducting the experience. I had signed Johanna and myself up as a couple for seventy five dollars for the five hour seminar. We left around six in the morning to go to a small town about thirty minutes east of Palmdale.

We got lost looking for the place but luckily we had left with enough time to spare. The address we had did not coincide with where the building should have been and were ready to just call it quits and drive back home when Johanna suggested that we just keep driving down the street. Finally we located the church at the end of the street, not at all where the address indicated it should be. At the seminar we learned how the whole Truth Project originated and the meaning behind it. I am amazed at the effect this program had on me, it was the jump start at the rebirth of my faith that really got me going. After spending the day around other people with the same focus I wanted to have, a biblical world view, it made me feel extraordinary.

Once we were on our way home I was just bursting at the seams about the experience. I wanted to get out and share this new product with everyone I knew. I actually thought this experience might be powerful enough to change my dad's outlook on his life and God. When we returned home we told Johanna's family about the experience and how great it was.

I ended up burning a copy for my grandma. She had heard me speak about my Wednesday nights and was excited to see what it was all about. I also burned a copy for my friend, Jarron, who I had played baseball with in college. He was at the time my only friend who was a Christian. I told him all about my rebirth and he was so proud of me because he had been around me when I did not have a relationship with God. He witnessed first hand the things I went through and the things I had done.

I still believe this DVD set helped solidify my relationship with Christ. I am forever grateful to that youth pastor who introduced me to the program. For anyone that is looking to help understand their own personal faith or for those who want to grow spiritually these movies are very useful tools. The power these videos have by bringing people together to speak about God and praise Him are fabulous. The videos are visually enticing and the way that Dr. Hackett speaks is profound to say the least. As you can tell I was thoroughly impressed even to this day with this collection of DVD's that are known as "The Truth Project."

In the meantime I wanted to throw a surprise party for Johanna for her birthday and to take this opportunity to propose to her. I talked to Michelle about helping me plan the party and told her to gather a list of people to invite. I went out looking for a place to have the party at, a place that would have to be extra special. I had driven by a restaurant a couple of time with Johanna in Woodland Hills that caught our eye because it had a giant gas torch outside that had a ten foot flame shooting out of it. The name of the restaurant was Roy's Hawaiian Cuisine and that is where I envisioned everything taking place.

I took a trip over to the restaurant and met with the coordinator. I told her my plans, then we looked at the banquet room and I knew this was the place. The lighting was dim to set the mood, the room was enclosed to make sure that we had privacy and by the cost on the menu I knew the food was going to be spectacular. I went ahead and booked the place for twenty five people and was given a menu to choose what I wanted to have served.

I left the restaurant and went over to Scott and Valerie's apartment to share with them my big plans for the party. I was looking through the menu of all of the delicious food and Scott was helping me pick. He told me how he thought the prices were high and if I was sure on the place. I told him that I didn't care what the price was because Johanna was worth whatever it cost. In the back of my mind I could envision the whole proposal plan where Scott just thought it was a birthday party. I talked to Michelle and she had given me a list of people to invite and the next thing to do was to get some invitations made up.

I didn't just want any invitations, I wanted them to be special. I decided to make them myself using Photoshop. I took a picture from the internet of a drawing of a red carpet event invitation and added the details. I took the picture and put Johanna's head on the cartoon bodied woman and then placed my head on the cartoon body of the guy who was stepping out of a limousine. I wrote on the back a note that said "you're invited to a party" and then the info for the party, at the bottom I made sure to include a note that said "shhh it's a surprise." I gathered up everyone's addresses and sent them out.

About a week later Johanna found out about the so called "surprise" party I was throwing for her and so it was changed to just a birthday party. We went out shopping for what we referred to as a "princess dress" for her downtown. She picked out a very beautiful pink dress I knew would look amazing on her. Along with the dress I bought her shoes and some jewelry so that she would look absolutely stunning. The both of us couldn't wait for the party to come, she couldn't wait for the party and I couldn't wait for the proposal. I could feel the anticipation building as the date drew nearer.

About this time Johanna's dad gave me a book that helped me out while in my current situation. The saying always goes "God works in mysterious ways" and this is one of those cases. No one told Reyes about what we were going through but he approached me one day and offered me a book to read. The book was about the struggles of the author and his sexual problems. The author couldn't stop looking at other women and couldn't stop fantasizing about them as well.

This book allowed me to understand I was not alone when it came to these types of problems. The book also offered a variety of tools to help combat these problems but most of all it was the real life testimony from another man that touched me. The man demonstrated his relationship with God helped him become the man he always wanted to be and needed to be for his wife and family. The book emphasized the strengthening of a relationship with God. Also, how important it was to succumb to the fact there was a problem and God's help was needed to restore everyday life.

On Wednesday May 20th my sister Melissa graduated from California State University of Northridge, The whole family attended her graduation and we all went to dinner afterwards. I couldn't believe how fast my little sister had grown up into a woman. I remember when she was just a little girl and now she had a four year old daughter Jordan around the same age as I remember her. After dinner I decided to leave my truck with Johanna so that she could use it to go back home and then to work. She didn't have a car at this time and I found it easier to just go home with my parents. My plan was to have her come out to visit me or I would catch a ride down to her house that weekend.

The next morning I received a phone call from the sales associate at Robbins Brothers who told me the ring I had ordered had come in early and was ready for pick up. I was so excited. Then she asked if I could pick it up before Saturday so the commission she would receive for the sale would be on her next paycheck. I agreed to come down the next day, which was Friday.

Now my mission was to somehow get down the San Fernando Valley without Johanna thinking anything was up. I called her and told her I had talked to Barzin and he wanted me to come down the next day to meet with him. So I told her I would take the Metrolink, a local train down to her house. She protested and didn't quite understand why I didn't want to wait until I had a ride. I somehow talked my way into taking the Metrolink and convincing her I would walk to her house from the station, which was only about a mile away to pick up my truck.

This is where the fun began. I had my sister, along with my niece Jordan, take me to the train station around seven in the morning. I boarded the train and was reading my book that Johanna's dad had let me borrow about how the world is so sexual and how to keep focused on the woman in your relationship. While reading the book it helped me put things in perspective about another man's struggle and how I saw what I didn't want to go through, or put Johanna through. The train ride was kind of relaxing and was something I had never done before so it was a little exciting.

As the train was entering the San Fernando Valley I noticed we were not going through the part of town where the station by Johanna's house was, instead we were going in a different direction. This whole time my mind is telling me it would just be a matter of time before the train would make a right turn and head in the direction of my destination. After it was apparent the train was not going to make any kind of turns to head in the direction of my destination is when I had to resort to a new plan.

After I frantically looked for the map of the stations I noticed that the train I was on did not go to the station by Johanna's house. I got off of the train at the next stop. The stop was about fifteen miles from Johanna's house and I was pressed for time. I still had to get in my car and drive to Robbins Brothers and was quickly running out of time. I called Johanna and told her about the predicament I was in and she told me to wait there until she went on her lunch and she would pick me up. I told her I had to meet Barzin and I didn't want to wait that long.

I ended up walking about two miles to get to a shopping center before I called a taxi to pick me up. I called the sales associate at Robbins Brothers but found out she was meeting me at that time in the store because it was her day off. I asked if they could reschedule our time to meet and they told me they would take care of it. Johanna was not happy with my decision to walk and catch a taxi at all.

When the taxi arrived it was a minivan and I knew then I wasn't going anywhere fast. The driver asked me where I wanted to go and he decided to take the most roundabout way to get there. I think it took about forty-five minutes and it cost me fifty dollars! I was relieved to finally reach the house and pick up my truck just to get back on the road again. When I arrived at the store I was tired from running around all morning. All of my hectic morning thoughts dissipated when I saw the ring. The ring was even more amazing in person than I could ever have imagined. I was floored by its beauty. I quickly finalized the deal and then left out the door with the ring in my hand.

Now the secret I had been keeping, except I did tell Kevin, all of this time was going to be harder because I had the actual hardware in my hand. I had to pick up Michelle from school that day and I couldn't help but tell her about my whole plan. After she was in the car for two minutes I revealed the box and when she opened it her face lit up. She commented on how pretty it was and then there was a pause. She stayed quiet for about a minute and then said "wait is that an engagement ring?" I told her that it was and she replied "Oh my gosh I think I am going to cry." I proceeded to spill my guts about my plan to propose at Johanna's birthday dinner and I told Michelle she was the only one who knew about it. I knew she could keep the secret because of the magnitude of it and the surprise would be that much better if she did.

I began working for Barzin on the last Monday in May. I drove down with all of my tools and was ready for a full days work. I began by taking down a portion of the wall to put in a doorway. It started off smoothly; I measured the doorway out and scored the line with a razor knife. Then I began using my hammer to punch holes through the wall to pull down the drywall. About halfway down the wall is when I hit my first snag. There was an electrical line along with a telephone line running across where the doorway was going to be. It took me a moment to think about what I was going to do about it. I never liked anything to do with electrical and to this day still hate anything to do with electrical work.

I ended up continuing what I was doing and removed all of the drywall. I began putting the wall back together with fresh drywall. Still unsure of what to do about the electrical and telephone lines passing through the doorway. I finally figured that since the line was only supplying one outlet I would just cut the line and cap it.

When this was decided I went back and cut the power to that side of the office. I crossed my fingers and then cut the line and capped it off. After restoring power to that side of the office I quickly discovered that the outlet that I thought the power had been cut too was still live. This perplexed me and then I tested the other outlets that were supposed to be live and they were dead. It turns out where I thought the power was flowing to was actually where the power was coming from. Now I was in trouble. I put a coat of mastic on the drywall for it to dry while I went to Home Depot to buy some wiring and electrical supplies.

When I came back I tried to play it off that I knew what I was doing. But I really was just experimenting at that time. I was unfamiliar about the fire codes for electricity and the changing of outlets. Most importantly I had no clue where it was acceptable and unacceptable to run wiring. I ended up deciding to run the wiring under the flooring. Which I know now to be a huge no-no. My job looked pretty bad, I had this beautifully constructed wall that looked great but then there was an electrical line that was running across the floor. I left for the night only feeling slightly bad about how I left the construction I was doing.

I arrived the next morning and quickly received a phone call from Barzin saying the way I left everything was unacceptable. I didn't cover anything up with plastic and now there was dust everywhere. I explained to him I had just taken down a wall of course there was going to be some dust. Then he told me one of the phones wasn't working. I told him I was aware of it and I would have it fixed today. I started to fool around with the electrical work that I had done so of course I had to cut the power. I warned everyone the power would be down for about ten minutes and to let me know when they were ready for the shutdown. After I received the okay from everyone I cut the power and began trying to fix my botched electrical job.

About five minutes into my work I received a phone call from Barzin telling me I had cut the power to one of his staff's computers. Apparently the girl wasn't smart enough to know that when I cut the power her computer was going to shutdown due to the fact it runs on electricity. He told me I couldn't be doing stuff like that and I needed to turn the power back on immediately. I expressed I couldn't do my job without the power being off. His response was I would need to come back later. So I packed up my stuff and left after only being there for about twenty minutes.

I waited for Barzin to call me and when he did the next day he told me he had to call in an electrician to fix the job I had done and that it cost him about two hundred dollars for the electrician. He told me my work was unacceptable. If the place burned down due to my faulty electrical work he would not have been covered under his insurance. He told me how much of a chance he had taken on me and how much of a liability I had become. I told him that I would just take the payment for what I had done and we would go our separate ways.

He promptly went out and hired another company and then proceeded to email me pictures of the work that they were doing all the while telling me how professional they were. I was so glad I had ended my agreement with him and it took nearly five months to finally receive only a portion of what he owed me. I did learn a valuable lesson in that I should always check things out before I just dive right in. On my walk through I should have punched a hole in the wall and made sure I was aware of what was behind the wall. Assuming that since there was no outlet there were no electrical lines was a lesson that cost me the job.

9

Miracles

I was still looking for work and in the mean time I was still doing odd jobs for Johanna's parents. Michelle's graduation from high school was on a Thursday and she wanted a party at the house in the backyard on that Saturday. The backyard needed some work and it was decided to put in sprinklers and lay some sod. I began work on the sprinklers and had them put in within two days. Then the measuring of the yard was done and the order for the sod was placed. The sod was put in on the Wednesday, the day before Michelle's graduation. Johanna's dad, Reyes, helped me lay all of the grass and we finished in two hours then rested from being out in the heat. The backyard looked really nice with the grass in and their dog Copper loved rolling around in it.

That Saturday Reyes woke up with some pain in his chest. It was decided we would take him to Valley Presbyterian hospital as a precautionary measure. Johanna had worked as a receptionist in the ER at the hospital for about a month and a half and still knew people there. I walked in after parking the car and Johanna was at the window seeing if she could have her dad seen as fast as possible. They called Reyes in after about five minutes, Maria joined him.

Michelle, Johanna and I waited in the emergency waiting room. I tried my best to reassure them he would be okay because God was watching over him and he had much more to do in his lifetime. I said prayers to comfort his family and for them not to worry. A while later Maria came back out with the doctor and told us that he had in fact had a heart attack and they were sending him up to surgery. The surgery was to place stents in the arteries to open them up. Johanna and Michelle went back to see their dad before he went up to surgery. I prayed the surgery would go well and everything would be okay. Within an hour of when we arrived at the hospital he was going into surgery.

We all waited for the surgery to be complete, and we continued to pray. When the surgery was over the doctor came out and said everything had gone extremely well. God was looking over Reyes that day and showed us just how precious life is. But he wasn't out of the woods just yet. When Reyes awoke everyone was by his hospital bed to shower him with love. He spent a few days in the hospital and was then released. He was given the choice to either have a couple more stents placed in other partially blocked arteries or he could opt for open heart bypass surgery to replace the blocked arteries with good arteries from his arm and leg.

When Reyes came home from the hospital he was in stable condition because the stents were in place. He would have to recover from the minor stent placement surgery before he could have another procedure done. We all were glad to have him home and thanked God for keeping him safe. He was in my prayers not only to keep him safe but to also give him guidance on what path to go down for his future decision on what surgery to have. I was scared for him having the open heart surgery because of his diabetes. Whenever the topic came up I voiced my opinion in the opposite direction, I wanted him to have more of the stents put in.

I kept praying about finding a job and then it happened. I received a phone call from my brother who told me there was an opening for a temporary RIS administrator at the Kaiser West Los Angeles facility. My eyes lit up like a kid on Christmas morning, my prayers had been answered. I found out the details and immediately put the finishing touches on my resume. Scott told me that he knew some people over there and would put in a good word for me. I submitted my resume on the website and he introduced me to the PAC's administrator named Jon. Scott told me I should listen to Jon, because he knew people there and Jon was pulling for me to get the job and that he would be a great help to me.

I called Johanna and told her about the possibility of a job opening at Kaiser in West Los Angeles and she was so excited. We began praying about how thankful we both were for this job opportunity to have arisen. I prepared as much as possible for the interview and when the call finally came in about the date and time of my interview I was more than ready. Scott told me about Arlene. She was the Director for the Radiology department and how nice she was. Scott kept reassuring me the job was pretty much mine; I wanted to believe him but didn't want to get my hopes up either. I continued to pray this job would turn into a permanent job. Or at least open the door to another job within Kaiser. Once on the inside I would be able to apply for permanent jobs before the public would be able to do so.

I didn't know the interview I was being called for was only a preliminary interview, done by the Human Resources department. After I was cleared I was called to schedule an interview for the Radiology department. I went on my interview and was confident this job was mine, unless I screwed up royally. I waited in the lobby in my suit and tie until I was called in to a back conference room. I sat across the table from the assistant director and Jon, the PAC's administrator, who I had met one time before.

Throughout the interview a couple of other people stopped in. The previous director Larry, who was now hired on as a consultant, asked me a few questions. Also the CAT scan tech, Jeremy, who was taking on much of the duties of the RIS administrator in the absence of one, asked me a few more questions. Arlene never did show up for the interview. When I left I felt as though the job was mine. I was already planning on how well I would have to perform to make this job a permanent one.

About a week later Johanna and I met up with my mom, dad, Melissa, Jordan, Scott and Valerie to go on a cruise to Mexico for my mom's sixtieth birthday. While we were all waiting to board the cruise ship in San Diego I received a phone call to tell me that I had been selected for the job. I was given on offer of $54,600 as an annual salary. Even though this was lower than my previous job, I was overjoyed to have been selected for the job. I figured if I became a permanent employee I would receive a raise and everything would be just fine. I quickly turned around and hugged Johanna and told her the great news. To see the sigh of relief in her eyes was all I needed to see to know everything would be just fine.

As I embraced her we both looked at each other and thanked God for His blessing. He had heard all of our prayers.

We never lost our faith in Him that he would take care of us and provide for us, even though he tested it with the timing. I no longer had to stress out about income even though I was scheduled to receive my very last check from my unemployment benefits in two weeks.

We had so much fun on the cruise. Neither of us had ever been on a cruise so it was perfect, we were able to go on our first together. The food was amazing, the atmosphere was lively and relaxing. When we stopped in port in Mexico we went shopping. Johanna's Spanish came in handy as she was able to secure many deals with her bartering skills. I really enjoyed being able to spend the days with my family. And even though I had been dating her for ten months, my family was able to get to know her a little better over the course of the cruise.

It was now July third, two-thousand nine and today would be the big day. I was going to sit down and ask Johanna's parents permission to marry their daughter. I was nervous. Not to talk to them or ask them for their daughter's hand in marriage. But because of the fact I had just gotten a job but not started yet. I told Reyes and Maria I wanted to speak with them and they agreed. I followed Reyes and Michelle down to Maria's work so we could talk there and then I could leave for home. I remember I wasn't nervous until I got into my truck by myself and began to follow them down. I said a little prayer to calm my nerves. Then I began going over what I was going to say out loud. I must have tried twenty different ways of saying what I wanted to say. I finally decided upon the one that I thought sounded the best and rehearsed it one last time before parking.

I waited until Reyes returned with Maria and they motioned for me to come out of my car and talk. They chose to sit on a bench located on the east side of the now vacant Century City Hospital building. This was a reminder to me of how God had always had a plan for me since the beginning. He was instrumental in me landing the position at the hospital and now he was bringing me back to ask permission to marry my dream girl that He so carefully placed in my life. I walked over and took a seat positioning myself side saddle so that I could speak to them more directly. Reyes was sitting on the outside and Maria on the inside closest to me, I really think they had no idea what was about to hit them.

I began by telling them over the last ten months of my dating Johanna I had fallen deeply in love with her. I expressed how I knew she was the only girl for me. Then I smoothly slipped in the question, “I brought the both of you here today to ask permission to ask Johanna to marry me.” When I finally said the words out loud it made me smile from ear to ear. I looked over and Reyes had a smile on his face, I think Maria was smiling inside but the first thing she told me was "marriage is a serious thing." I told her I knew that and then both of them talked to me about how much they liked me and they knew Johanna loved me.

They both wanted to make absolutely sure I knew what I was getting into.

After about a five minute discussion Maria asked me if I had a ring yet? I told her I did and then I told them I wanted to propose to her at her birthday party the following weekend. They granted me permission and Maria opened her arms and said "welcome to the family." I felt such a sigh of relief. Now everything was prepared and ready. The only thing left to do was to plan the proposal itself and what I would say to Johanna.

The day finally arrived. This would be a moment that we wouldn't forget and would be imprinted in our minds forever. If everything went as planned then she would be as happy as could be and say "Yes!" I knew this would be extra special because I was asking her in front of all of the people that were special in her life and mine. I wanted to do it this way as opposed to a one on one type of proposal. I knew how important her family is to her and my family is very important to me as well. I prayed everything would go accordingly and God would give me the right words to say and keep me calm in doing so. The morning started off with Johanna going and getting her hair and nails done in preparation for the big night.

The party was on Saturday July eleventh and started at five. We left and made it about twenty minutes early. The coordinator met me and almost spilled the beans about the proposal because she didn't think Johanna was there yet. She was still under the impression it was a surprise party. I had to quickly divert a possible implosion of my well thought out plan and walk away with the coordinator. After I told her then we were set to go.

People started showing up while appetizers were being served. As the room filled up I started to get a little nervous but it was the good nerves. I think I was more anxious than anything. I kept all of this inside and had done so much planning and organizing just for this one night to be as memorable as possible. I wanted to obviously wait until everyone arrived before I popped the question but I wasn't sure whether to do it before or after dinner. I decided I would do it as soon as the last person arrived but before dinner was served. A few people were late so the waiting game played with my nerves a little bit. I tried to keep reminding myself this would all go smoothly because I had God's blessings.

When we first arrived at the restaurant I handed the ring off to Michelle, but now I asked for it back so that I could get prepared for the moment. I took a moment to calm down and recite exactly what I would say. Then I turned to Johanna and told her that we should stand up and thank everyone for coming, she agreed. We both stood up and I was so excited that she still had no clue what was about to happen. I had only let a couple people in on the surprise, my brother so he could video the event and Chase so he could shoot some pictures of it.

We stood up and addressed everyone and told them how thankful we were they were able to make it. Then I turned to Johanna and told her how much I loved her and I want to ask her a question, "Will you marry me?" I reached into my pocket and produced a box that contained a ring that was especially made for her. She quickly covered her mouth and began to cry, I remember hearing my brother tell me to get down on one knee. I went to my knee and she said "Yes!" I stood up and we hugged and kissed. I pulled the ring out of the box and placed it on her finger, in my opinion a ring never looked more at home than it did on her finger.

The rest of the night was like a fairytale, the food was great and everyone's spirits were high. This was the life changing event I had been waiting for. I knew in my mind this would right our ship. We both expressed how blessed we were from God to be able to have each other. This part of my life was a real eye opener for me, to show me how wonderful and glorious God was. It was like we were coming out of a storm on the ocean with nothing but clear skies and calm waters ahead. It was hard for both of us to sleep that night. We spent the whole night talking about how much we loved each other and how happy the other one made us. The next step was to plan the actual wedding.

Reyes decided on having the bypass surgery and it was scheduled on the Monday following Johanna's party. This was a quick turn of emotions for the family, it went from extreme elation of our engagement to being worried about this major surgery the male figure in the family was to have. I was glad I chose to propose to Johanna before Reyes' surgery because I was hoping it gave him a little peace of mind that I was there to help watch over and take care of his family while he would not be able to.

The surgery was early in the morning so we all packed into two cars and drove down to Cedar Sinai hospital in Los Angeles. I remember on the way down we took a canyon road and it was a little foggy and off on the side of a road we saw a deer standing by the edge of the road. Since that day I have probably taken that canyon road over fifty times and I have yet to see another deer. I believe it was God's way of reminding us how beautiful and precious life is. I think it was just a reminder of his presence and to let us know he was watching over Reyes.

When we arrived at the hospital we followed Reyes until he had to go off by himself. He turned and gave everyone hugs and reassured us he would be all right. We all waited in the waiting room and Johanna wanted me to reassure her that everything would be alright. I told her God was watching over her dad and He wouldn't let anything happen to him. The surgery took a long time, every couple of hours a nurse would come out and give us an update about his status. Once the surgery was over the doctor came out and told us everything went well but they were having a little trouble stopping his bleeding because he was diabetic.

After they were able to stop the bleeding he was sent to the recovery room. Maria stayed by his side even though he was not awake she wanted to be there when he did come to. I felt sad inside for Maria because I couldn't imagine going through such an ordeal with the person I love the most. Most of the time I tried to be upbeat and positive and stay focused on the fact that God was watching over Reyes.

Sometimes I let my emotions get the best of me. I would think about what it would be like to have to go through that with my dad or with my spouse. It saddened me deeply to think those thoughts. Johanna was strong for her mom and for Michelle but she would break down when it was just me and her alone and I was glad to be the one there to comfort her and reassure her everything would be just fine. I think going through that helped us put things in a different perspective and it made our relationship grow.

I was blessed in the fact that I received my job when I did. By the time my last unemployment benefit check ran out I was starting my first day of orientation for Kaiser. Thankfully Johanna's parents were so kind that they were going to let me stay at their house while I was working down in Los Angeles. I offered to pay them four hundred dollars a month and help out with as much as I could around the house while Reyes was making his recovery.

I gathered up my clothes and moved down to Johanna's room. She would switch off from sleeping in the living room on the couch or on a mattress, while sometimes sharing a bed with her sister. This was such a blessing because Johanna was going to school and I was the only one working and it allowed me to save more money for the wedding. Johanna had quit her job as an assisted living apartment manager because the company had broken the contractual agreement to give her, her own apartment to live in. She made the decision to go to school full time to finish her pre-requisites so she would be able to be accepted into the nursing program. I totally supported the idea and encouraged her to focus solely on school.

About this time is when we started to talk about the time frame for the wedding. We both didn't see the need for a long engagement and decided a six month window would allow us enough time to plan and coordinate everything. One of the drawbacks was my job was only a six month temporary position. I was fully convinced God would take care of us and allow either the position to become permanent or he would open another door for me. We decided that the wedding would be in January and I didn't think it would be a problem. My mom wanted me to ask Scott and Valerie if it was okay to get married so close to their wedding. They were both okay with the idea as long as we didn't use any of the same colors as they were planning on using. So it was set. A January wedding.

As things about our wedding preparations were stirring in my head I started orientation for work on the Monday after Reyes had his surgery. I was so excited to start my new job, I knew from speaking with people in the department that things were a mess, but I didn't know how badly just yet. I knew things were going to be bad when all throughout my week of orientation I was told by people they were glad I was here, and they couldn't wait for me to start. I started training the following Monday at my own facility and then went and trained for a couple of days in Woodland Hills.

Within my first two weeks of working for Kaiser I decided to purchase a new vehicle. There was a stimulus program implemented by President Obama called the "Cash for Clunkers" event. The program allowed people with cars or trucks that got bad gas mileage to trade in their vehicles for a more fuel efficient vehicle. If the trade in vehicle had a difference of ten or less miles to the gallon of gas then the person received three-thousand five hundred dollars for their trade in. If the trade in vehicle had a difference of more than ten miles to the gallon of gas the person received four thousand five hundred dollars for their trade in. With my big Yukon Denali getting only about thirteen miles to the gallon, I was in a position to trade it in for the maximum credit allowed.

My biggest reason for trading in the truck was it had one hundred and thirty thousand miles on it and it got really bad gas mileage. With the gas prices so high it was costing me over a hundred dollars to fill up my tank. The other thing was, I was spending a lot of time on the road with my new job. It was taking me forty five minutes to get to work and an hour to get back home, even though it was only about twenty miles away.

My whole family drives Hyundai cars. My dad was telling me how Hyundai's warranty couldn't be matched, it was a ten year or one hundred thousand mile warranty. I decided to take a look at some, but I knew I wanted an SUV instead of a car. Johanna and I went to the Hyundai dealership on Van Nuys Blvd after I came home from work one night to look at what was available. I decided that I liked the Santa Fe which was a mid-sized SUV. After discussing prices for a while we decided on a slightly used one that was a year old with only eleven thousand miles on it. The car itself was in pristine condition, it had been used by the dealership manager to travel. We spent sometime discussing financing and pricing and finally finished the deal around ten at night. I had traded in my truck for a more efficient and more reliable vehicle, I was proud of my decision.

Back at work everyone was right, everything was a complete mess. For the first week I was completely swamped. Not only was I trying to learn the system but fix all of the outlying problems that existed before I arrived. It took about two full months to finally get caught up and have things start to run smoothly. After I was caught up from the previous work and was only focusing on maintaining the system, things came very easily for me. I fixed so many problems and worked to get things straightened out and to be made more efficient.

Part of the problem was the person in the position before me was not only the RIS administrator but also the assistant director of the department. She was spread very thin and ultimately did not give the amount of attention needed to the RIS system. This made me look awesome when I came in. I received so much praise from top to bottom in the department; everyone was thoroughly impressed with my hard and diligent work.

The whole time I was working both myself and Johanna were praying for my job to become a permanent one so most of our problems would be solved. I could tell by all of the praise I was receiving for how much better things were since I arrived, that I just knew my position would become a permanent one.

Reyes was still improving daily and it was a miracle to watch his recovery progress so fast. We prayed nightly for his recovery to go smoothly and rapidly. God heard our prayers because he was up walking around in no time. I was helping out with as much as I could around the house, I would mow the lawn and do the yard work or take out the garbage. These were small tokens of my gratitude and I was so thankful I had such a beautiful family to live with and care for me as well.

10

Building for the Future

When I moved in I began attending church with Johanna and her family for the early service at The Church on the Way. This was a massive church with about twenty-thousand members. The church was divided between the English side and the Spanish side. Her family went to the Spanish side so I did as well. I was given an ear piece to listen to the service through a translator and I would pick up words to add to my Spanish vocabulary. I enjoyed going to worship every Sunday at eight, it allowed for a group event for the family to bond. The sermons were delivered well, by connecting our lives today with teachings from the Bible. My favorite part about the service was the music; they had about a nine or ten instrument band with about six singers. I enjoyed singing in Spanish mostly because it allowed for me to read, speak and understand Spanish at a much slower pace.

After church was over we would go back home and start our day. I liked going to the early service because by the time we were out of church we had the whole day to be productive. I always felt as though I was refreshed, cleansed and re-energized to go about the day with a biblical outlook on what I had planned. I would like to think that this feeling would last me throughout the entire week but most of the time it wouldn't. It is so important to have other activities during the week to remain focused.

This whole time between me working, Johanna going to school and her dad's recovery from bypass surgery we were still trying to save and plan for our wedding. We both knew we wanted to be married in the church so that was a no brainer. The reception hall was chosen after seeing a few others. We both came to the agreement that for the money and location this was the best deal. We decided on Porter Valley Country Club and placed a down payment to reserve Saturday January 23rd. We went to a bridal show one weekend and got some ideas, mostly about how expensive everything was. All the while I was still selling baseball cards and my goal was to raise ten thousand dollars for the wedding. I had a pretty good business on EBay selling baseball cards. I was bringing in somewhere in the neighborhood of two to four hundred dollars a week.

Being newly engaged we wanted to take engagement pictures to be able to share with family and friends. I was able to score a very talented and well taught photographer by the name of Chase Dominguez to take our pictures. We traveled up to Tehachapi one Saturday to take the pictures. Chase took us up into the mountains for some beautiful pictures with the scenery around us. With those pictures done I also wanted to do a few of my own. What would engagement pictures be if I didn't have a hand in them?

I picked the location of our first encounter, Century City Doctor's Hospital. Now that the hospital was closed down it was not hard to arrange this. I took a couple of amazing pictures. One is of us embracing each other with the Century City street sign in the background and the other was a little more involved. The picture is a multiple exposure shot of us running towards each other and finally meeting in the middle with me holding Johanna up in the air. The thing that also makes this shot unique is I superimposed a picture of us staring into each other's eyes in the background.

On August 21st Johanna and I celebrated our one year anniversary. It was a great time to just reflect upon all we had gone through and where we were now in our relationship. As I reflected I couldn't believe all of the trials and tribulations the Lord had put us through to get us on the path we needed to be on. I felt that we were not totally where we wanted to be but at least we were now on the right path to get to where we wanted to be. I was truly happy with my future wife and was so excited to plan our wedding and our future together. This milestone was made more special by the fact that our relationship was connected to God and through Him we would flourish with each other.

For our one year anniversary I gave Johanna a set of Wilson golf clubs that were pink. My hope was to get her interested in golf so I could have a golf partner for life. The experiment was well received and she was excited to get out and play. I told her we would have to take steps before we could just go out and play. We would have to go to the driving range a few times and then start off small at the par three courses, before moving up. I was a little afraid she wouldn't have the patience for it but she proved otherwise.

The next morning we were meeting with our second florist, after the first one turned out to be a little too pricey. I will be the first to tell you I had no idea how much flowers cost. I bought flowers for Johanna many times and ordered her some to be delivered a couple times, but that was no way to estimate how much flowers would cost. I was floored the first time we met with a florist and found out that she wanted to do our wedding for around three-thousand dollars. So when we met with this florist I was made a little more price conscious.

We met the florist, Leah, in her home and started going over flower choices, flower arrangements, colors and cost. She was very nice and seemed to know a lot about flowers and wanted to tailor everything to what we wanted. We decided to go with her and agreed on a price around fifteen-hundred dollars. I think this was the first moment I realistically thought our budget was going to be an unobtainable number.

The following week we had our dinner tasting at Porter Valley Country Club. We drove up after I got out of work. We were ushered into a side room where a two person table was set up. As we sat down the gentleman overseeing our event introduced himself and told us he would take care of us. Then we were ready to try our food. We had the opportunity to taste a few different appetizers, a couple of salads and a couple of entrees.

When it came time to order our entrees I wanted the Cordon Bleu and Johanna ordered a mushroom chicken. When my Cordon Bleu came it was so delicious I could hardly contain myself. The choices were made and the Cordon Bleu was hands down the choice for the entree. We left our food tasting full and satisfied with the decisions we made.

We found out from the church we had to attend a twelve week program for pre-marital couples. This class was a blessing due to the wealth of knowledge it provided about getting, being and remaining married. The classes were every Sunday for two hours and were held in a room upstairs from the church for the English side of our church. There were about six other couples that went through the program with us. The first class we attended I recognized the pastor that was conducting the classes as a guy I had seen at my dad's work. It turned out the Kodak rep my dad dealt with on a regular basis was conducting the class.

The class style was informative on a variety of topics that were troublesome in marriages of study. The main overall focus of the class was to show you without God in your marriage you would fail. The center of the marriage and more importantly the center of our lives needed to be focused on God. The class was taught by the Pastor and his wife and then every week would be a new topic with a new set of sub teachers that would teach on that individual topic. The couples that taught on individual topics were an interesting collection of people; they came from different backgrounds and different social and family situations.

The different varieties of couples played into the program, because it helped get the realism of what these people were talking about across to us. Most of the teachers had been through ordeals in their own marriages. They wanted to show us what not to do. If we did find ourselves in the same predicament then God was the answer to all of the problems. Every set of couples no matter how old or young had one thing in common, God. Whatever their own marriages went through whether it was financial problems, extra marital issues, drugs or alcohol issues or a wide variety of other issues God was always the answer. These couples showed us through their own testimonies how God answered their prayers.

Every week we would start the class off by praising God through worship and then go into the lesson at hand. The couples would then lead us in prayer before starting the lessons. Along with the classes we had homework to do outside of class. The homework involved reading books about topics in marriage that could be used as useful tools down the road. This class served many purposes for us as a couple, many topics were brought up we had not discussed or even thought about yet.

We were encouraged to stop having sex if we were. I had been feeling I was in the right spot in my life with Christ but I had a little blemish in the area of having pre-marital sex. So once we agreed to stop until the wedding night which was about eighteen weeks away I felt closer to God.

The class and the people involved were such a blessing to Johanna and me. We learned about all different scenarios we would probably encounter. Now given the right tools we could disarm many problems. We learned not only did we have to grow spiritually in God's eyes as a couple we still needed to maintain the balance of having our individual relationships with him as well. I am so thankful I had the opportunity to be a part of something so beautiful and helpful. I took away many useful tools I know I will use in my marriage in my future.

Over the next couple of months we both were adjusting to living with each other. The best part about our situation was that we were able to see each other all of the time and spend all of our time together. Unfortunately this was also the problem some of the time. We both are very stubborn and we both love to be right, while hating to be wrong. This period was an adjustment period to say the least. We would have our fights about who was right and who was wrong all of the time. Most of the time the fights we had were about things that didn't even matter one way or another.

One of the problems we were having was that I am a simple guy when it comes to details; on the other hand Johanna is like an investigative reporter. If we had a disagreement then I was completely content with finding a solution, a couple of "I am sorry's," a kiss, a hug and that was it. Johanna wanted to get to the bottom of it, she wanted to know why I did what I did, which is understandable, but sometimes she would take it too far. Her questioning after a while would drive me up the wall and I would start to ignore her. That would only make her more upset and the vicious cycle was in full effect.

After a while, sometimes hours, we would both come to our senses and look at what we had just done and realize how stupid it was. We loved each other and were getting married in a few months and yet we couldn't get along sometimes.

At this point in my life everything was starting to fall into place. It is an awesome feeling when you feel God's hand guiding you down the path He has created for you. My relationship with God was growing stronger everyday, my job security was looking great and I was scheduled to marry the girl of my dreams only a few months away in January. At this point we were instructed to become members of the church. One Sunday after class we stayed for another three hours for the new member's class. We learned where the church originated and what the plans for the future entailed. I really thought the class was too impersonal. It made me feel as though I was just another person to add to the list of others. The pastor teaching the class was going through all the material at a supersonic speed. When we were done with the class I was left feeling empty from the experience.

The following Wednesday, which was November 11th, was the day Johanna and I decided to get baptized. We arrived at the church and were met by the pastor who would assist with the baptizing. I was anxious because I had wanted this for a while and now the opportunity was here. What was even better was the fact that my future wife was going to go through the same process as I was.

All of the people who were to be baptized gathered in a room upstairs and we were accompanied by the pastor who would be performing the baptism. He went through the process and preached about the importance of being baptized. He gave us the story behind why we get baptized and the biblical story about John the Baptist. Afterwards he prayed with and for us. He explained how baptism symbolized the dying to self and coming alive in Jesus. And how the church practiced full immersion baptism because by being fully buried beneath the water we symbolize that God's grace fully fills us with His new life for the future. Through baptism we are truly born again in Jesus.

The men and the women were split up to go to the changing rooms. I was the only man that night being baptized along with Johanna and four other girls. I went into the dressing room and changed into a blue smock. Once I was done changing I stood in the changing stall and prayed to have my heart opened and ready to receive all that was given to me. I exited the room and stood in the hallway with Johanna and the other people. We looked at each other and held one another while we waited. As we got the signal to move into the pool I gave her a kiss and we began moving forward. I remember the pool water was warmer than I expected but it had a strong chlorine smell coming from it.

Once we were in the water we were able to look out into the people in the church. The pastor conducting the service announced our baptism and then told the congregation to bow their heads to pray for us. After his prayer we began. I moved towards the pastor performing the baptism and he told me to place my hands across my chest and plug my nose. He stood next to me and prayed for me. About this time is when it seemed that time was moving slower.

I remember praying over and over again to clear my mind and open my heart. Once the pastor's prayer concluded he started to lean me back, I bent my knees and he dunked my head under water. With such grace he started me back up again and I was standing up in the water, I moved towards the steps to exit the pool. I remembering feeling a warm sensation all over my body. I believe that is when the Holy Spirit entered my body and was now more present than ever.

I was handed a towel as I exited the pool and I waited for Johanna. I was dripping wet and when Johanna came up the steps and we both hugged one another and I felt our bond with God was stronger now then ever before. We went our separate ways to change back into our clothes and then we met up back in the room we had started in. We sat for a moment on the couch together and held hands both looking at each other with big smiles. I think our hearts were gracious that we had made it this far and were smiling at each other as well. The pastor came into the room and he prayed with us about our experience. On our way out he gave us a book on being re-birthed.

That Saturday we attended the new member's dinner for the church. We brought Kentucky Fried Chicken to the pot luck and were surrounded by fellow new members with all sorts of different kinds of food. After everyone had a chance to eat and socialize at their own tables. Then the pastor stood up in front of the room to speak. He was speaking to us about why we came to church and what the purpose was.

He started going around the room and asking people when they started attending the church and how they came to this church. I was positioned right in front of him and he looked down and asked me to stand up and tell everyone my story of why I chose this church. I was a little caught off guard, but I was pleased to offer my story. I told him I had come to the church because my beautiful soon to be wife brought me not only to the church but to the Lord as well. He was impressed. He looked at Johanna and told her there is a special place in heaven for bringing me to the Lord. Everyone in the room clapped and I felt really good about myself.

11

The News

About this time I received my giant shipment of baseball cards from Beckett Grading Services. I went through my collection of unopened sets that I kept in a chest big enough that I could crawl into. I pulled out all of the cards I thought would make me more money if I had them graded. I ended up sending in one-hundred cards at five dollars a piece. When I got the shipment back I was ecstatic because this was money that could now be easily obtained due to the fact that graded cards sell better on EBay. I wished all of these cards I was going to sell would be staying in my collection but at the time it just wasn't possible. I ended up selling the cards for close to two-thousand dollars and putting that money into our wedding fund.

Every week was filled with things to do for the wedding. By this time Johanna was excelling at golf, I couldn't believe how fast she had picked it up. Her chipping was amazingly good for a beginner, and she was pretty good off the tee as well. Overall she was better than I anticipated for how many times she had gone. I was so proud of her and told all of my friends how good she was. Some of her highlights included a par in her second round, a one hundred and eighty yard drive within her first ten rounds and a birdie attempt in about round number twelve. I was so thankful that she had embraced the game and loved to play golf. This made it easy to just go to the range or play a round whenever we felt like it.

When December rolled around I was nicely locked into my routine at work and at home. I was quickly approaching my thirtieth birthday and I was not excited about it. I have always hated getting older it makes me sad thinking about where all of the years went. It is funny when I was younger I couldn't wait to be older and now I am older I wish I was younger. I was dreading thirty because I felt as though I wasn't where I wanted to be when I imagined myself at thirty. But as I broke it down I was doing just fine. I had a good job and I was going to be married in about a month. If Johanna finished school when she planned, then when I was about thirty-two we would start our family and all would be great.

I started talking to Johanna about moving to a place where I could afford to buy a home and where there would be a good neighborhood to raise a family. I kept telling Johanna I wanted to move back to Nebraska but I knew that would never happen. I started pushing Tehachapi. Johanna had never lived anywhere else besides with her parents and after twenty-four years she had grown really attached.

I was glad Johanna had never moved out on her own and I would be the first person she ever lived with. I thought it would be a very special moment and I felt privileged to be the one to share it with her. I told her we could save our money by staying with her parents for about a year. Hopefully in that time period a job opening would open up at another Kaiser facility that would allow us to move. At least after a year we would have enough money to live in an apartment and continue searching for a house. She was okay with the plan because she too wanted her own home. She thought it would be a great idea to live with her parents while she was still in school, to help us out.

My birthday came and it was not as bad as I imagined it in my mind. All of the worrying I did was for nothing because I realized as long as I kept my faith strong then God would always take care of me. Johanna wanted to take me out for dinner and we decided on Chi Chi's Pizza, which is one of my favorites if not my favorite place to eat. When we arrived we went around the corner and my entire family was there to surprise me. I felt blessed I was able to share my thirtieth birthday with my family and Johanna. She really did surprise me and it made me cherish the fact she is my everything and how much I truly do love her.

About a week later I had a training session with the RIS administrator for Panorama City Kaiser. This day was an example of how I know God is watching over me and guiding me through life. While I was there training my counterpart from the facility decided to take a break so we headed for the break room. As we entered the break room he introduced me to the PAC's Administrator and a project manager for the facility. We were all sitting around the table making small talk and I found out that the project manager knew my mom and dad. They were also talking about my brother being the PAC's administrator over at Kaiser Sunset when all of a sudden the project manager brought up a RIS administrator position in Bakersfield.

Bakersfield is about forty-five minutes west of Tehachapi so I was immediately interested and asked if they had found anyone yet. The project manager explained to me how they were looking for someone but they couldn't find anyone that wanted to move out there. I cut her off and told her with a dead serious face "I have been looking for something out there, because I want to move out that way." She gave me the name of the director of radiology so I could get in contact with him. I sent him an email telling him I was interested in the job.

I finished my training which was only about another hour and then left. Since Kaiser Panorama City was only about three minutes away from Johanna's parents house I waited until I got home to tell Johanna about the exciting news. She was not nearly as excited as I was but excited nonetheless. She told me if it was something I was serious about and interested in, I should follow that and she would support and follow me. This was kind of a mini moment letting me know I was indeed marrying a very special woman who was extremely committed to me. This was perfect news that left me in a great mood to send me into the holidays.

The next day was Christmas Eve and I was so lucky that I would be able to celebrate Christmas with both Johanna's family and my family. Johanna's family celebrates Christmas at midnight on Christmas Eve, whereas my parents celebrate Christmas on the twenty-fifth. We stayed up until midnight on Christmas Eve and then we opened our gifts and had a wonderful time. Johanna bought me a sweet looking Guitar as my gift. The next day we went out to my parent's house and spent the day with my family. It was so much fun to watch my niece Jordan open up her gifts and it brought back endearing memories from when I was a kid.

I have always had a soft spot in my heart for Christmas time. I absolutely love it. Now I love Christmas for a different reason, sure the family and presents thing is fun too. It reminds me that God sent His only son Jesus down to earth to die for our sins. This is the day of my savior's birth and I am so thankful for it. I have Jesus to thank for my new life, without Him I would not have been forgiven for all of the sins I have done in my lifetime. I also enjoy spending quality time with my family, and it seems for one day at least everyone and everything is how they used to be.

Growing up I always had exceptional Christmas'. Around Christmas time I remember those memories and it makes me feel all warm and cozy inside. Christmas is also a time to reflect on what I have in life to be thankful for, I am so unbelievably thankful for Johanna and all she is. She is such an amazing person both inside and out.

After Christmas when I returned to work I decided I better get my resume in order if I was going to apply for this new job. I went through and updated my resume and prepared it to be submitted. On December 30th I submitted my resume for the RIS administrator job in Bakersfield. I received a message the next day from the director of the department telling me the human resource department would be looking over the applications and resumes and would be ready to schedule interviews sometime in the next two weeks. I didn't understand why I would have to interview for the position because I was the only RIS administrator I knew of from Kaiser applying for the job. I did find out since it was an exempt job they could hire anyone they wanted to. I am not a part of the union so I don't get the same benefits a union person would receive, but this job was available to anyone inside or outside the company.

After the New Year I was in preparation mode for the wedding. We were finalizing our details and guests for the event. We had to make arrangements for the guests we had coming in from out of town. Johanna and I were both anxious and stressed out from doing all of the planning and hoping everything went as planned. We had to figure out all of the hotel arrangements and a place for Justin Connors, who was staying with us, to sleep.

I received a call from the Human Resource department about setting up my interview for the job. I scheduled it for the fourteenth of January which was a Thursday. I told my current job that I had an appointment to go to and that I would be back after lunch. I woke up that morning and drove to Bakersfield with Johanna. She was looking out the window the whole time and at the clock. I knew that she didn't really want to move because of the distance from her parents and the fact that the wide open country scared her. I knew that if I could only get her to agree to the move she would fall in love with the countryside.

We finally arrived after almost two hours of driving to the Kaiser building where I was scheduled to have my interview.

Before I went in we prayed in the car, I asked God to have the right words for me to speak and calm my nerves. I walked into the building with my nice suit on and a boat load of confidence. I figured I already had a job so I really didn't have anything to lose. I felt my interview with the panel of six people went extremely well. When I got back to the car I told Johanna now the decision was in God's hands and we left to drive back down below.

I didn't have to wait long for an answer from the director of the department. He called me the following Monday only four days from when I interviewed. I was told, out of all of the candidates I was the most qualified and the committee all agreed I would be the best person for the job. Once I received the news I couldn't wait to tell Johanna the news. I called her and when she picked up I told her I got it. She was proud of me and started preparing mentally for the move. I was glad to get the news because the next day was my last day before I left for my vacation time from work for the wedding. I wanted to find out before the wedding so I would have that peace of mind going into the wedding not worrying about the job.

12

The Wedding

I was feeling anxious about the wedding. I had the same feeling as a kid would for Christmas, only ten times stronger. I wasn't nervous because I knew in my heart God had chosen Johanna as my wife. God not only calmed my nerves but also allowed my stress about planning to dissipate.

It had been raining since Monday and now on Wednesday I had to go pick up my friends at the airport. Johanna and I had been praying the day of the wedding would be clear and the rain would let up. The forecast did show rain and we did start to prepare for the fact that it could rain. We reassured each other that everything would be fine because both the ceremony and the reception were inside.

After picking up my friends from the airport we hung out and talked. Kevin and his wife Lindsey had flown in along with my other friend from Nebraska Justin Connors. I introduced them to Johanna because none of them had ever met her before, only heard stories from me about her. Having my friends meet my future wife brought a smile to my face because they now could put a person with the name. Now they would be able to see how special she was and see how much joy and happiness she brought to my life.

I thought if I kept myself busy with my friends in town I wouldn't stress about the wedding. We had planned on going golfing but with all of the rain it turned out to not be possible. Basically we just caught up on old times and hung out.

The next day was the day I had to pick up my college buddies Jared and Tyler Bain from the airport but their flight was cancelled due to all of the rain. Later that night was the rehearsal and the rehearsal dinner. Our rehearsal was at seven at night so we decided to have the dinner before the rehearsal. The dinner was at El Torito Mexican restaurant and everyone who was in the wedding party was invited.

It was a collection of people that were all close to us and supported us. I had my friends from Nebraska, my close friend

DJ and even my friend from Arizona, Chris Rubio, attend. We had a wonderful evening of food and socializing. We stood up and thanked everyone for coming and then we handed out gifts to the wedding party.

When it came to Johanna and me exchanging gifts I was excited to show her what I had for her. I wanted her to know how special she was and how much I was looking forward to her becoming my wife. I gave her a collage I made for her with all of the stationary from our invitations. I followed that gift up with a Tiffany's bracelet and a card expressing my feelings. She gave me a very unique gift of cufflinks made from a seat at the old Yankee Stadium. This gift blew me away because I could tell she had put a lot of thought into what she wanted to get me.

After, we all left the restaurant creating a convoy en route to the church. Before everyone arrived I met with the wedding coordinator to go over some final details. She asked me if I was comfortable with a prayer before we began. I agreed. When everyone arrived, she turned to me and asked if I would lead us in prayer before we began. I looked at her like I had no idea what she was talking about. Apparently there was a mix up. I thought she was asking if a prayer would be okay to do before we started, I didn't know she was asking me to lead the prayer.

She ended up leading us in prayer. As soon as she concluded her prayer I was upset I had not taken the opportunity to pray. This would have been the perfect time to show everyone in the room how far I had come. I wanted them to be encouraged by my ability to be proud of who I was and to take control in their own lives to find Jesus. I thought that this would have been the ideal setting for everyone to open their eyes and see the new me. I wish that I did things differently that day, but now I know to never let that opportunity pass me by again. God has a plan for me to reach out to everyone in that room that night, maybe this book will help start the process.

The rehearsal went smoothly without problems. Now all we had to do was to wait and hope the same happened on the wedding day. I felt the presence in the church that night of God and I left feeling his blessings for our wedding day.

The Lord did bless our wedding day because when I woke up on January 23rd, the rain had ceased and the sun was shining ever so brightly. My face was lit up with joy because I knew in my heart God was watching over us. After raining for about five days straight the rain was gone and we could have a nice clear day for our wedding.

I stayed the night at my brother Scott's apartment with my friend Justin. After waking up and having breakfast I didn't want to rush to just sit around and wait. I took a shower and shaved trying to take in the little things around me. I waited around for Scott and Justin to get ready before we left. I remember the time seemed to creep by so slowly that morning.

We arrived at the church around noon and were ushered into the dressing room. It was fun to have all of my closest friends in the same room all getting ready for the big moment. We all horsed around and told stories to break the tension. Scott was sitting at the table in the room copying down his best man toast for later on. I thought about writing down something but then I remembered the scene from the movie Wedding Crashers when Owen Wilson tells Rose McGown to speak from the heart. This is what I wanted to do, speak from my heart. I didn't need to write down how I felt about Johanna or what we went through because it was all in my heart.

After spending a while getting ready in the room the videographer arrived and began filming some scenes for the wedding video. A short while later the photographer came in and took us out in front of the church to take some pictures. As we walked back to the room I was still unusually calm for an event in which I thought I would be a nervous wreck. We waited for what seemed to be an eternity for people to start arriving at the church for the ceremony.

As I was coming down the homestretch the door opened to the dressing room and the wedding coordinator came in. She looked at me and told me she had bad news. I immediately thought something had happened to Johanna. She continued to tell me that in the twenty years she had been doing weddings this had never happened. I was starting to fear the worse. She told me the pastor was sick and they were lucky enough to find a replacement. My emotion changed from worried to a little upset that she had come in and presented the information the way she did.

The news was broken to me about forty-five minutes before the ceremony was set to begin. The replacement pastor entered the room and began talking to me about how I met Johanna and just some other small talk. At this point it was only Scott, the pastor and me in the room. Scott turned to me and said "it's all right if you are nervous". I told him I wasn't, I told him I was more nervous when I went on my job interview than I was right now. I prayed for God to open up my heart and clear my mind to be able to use all of my senses to remember every little detail that was about to take place. The door opened and we were told that it was time to make our entrance. I took a deep breath and walked out.

As I passed through the doorway the first thing I noticed was how beautiful the church looked. I thought to myself what a glorious setting for us to be married in God's eyes. I then focused my attention on the people in the room. I found my parents and smiled at them and then I found Johanna's mom and smiled at her. The whole time I was trying to focus on keeping a big smile so I looked good for the video and pictures.

When the doors in the back opened and the first people from the wedding party stepped through my bottom lip started to quiver. I was trying so hard to keep my smile going but my lip would not stop quivering. It felt like a dream. We had been planning and coordinating everything for so long and now I was in the middle of it, I couldn't believe it.

As soon as the doors closed back up again after the last person from the bridal party walked through I could hardly contain myself in anticipation. Then there was a moment of silence and the room was still. When the bridal march music started I took a deep breath and waited for the doors to open.

The doors opened and as I saw my beautiful bride for the first time it made my eyes well up with tears. She was walking down the aisle on her dad's arm and I watched our entire relationship flash before my eyes up until that moment. As she was getting closer our eyes met and I was lost in them. We had a connection for a minute that we just knew what each other were thinking through our eyes. Reyes made the handoff and then we bowed our heads in prayer. This allowed me to wipe my eyes and regain my composure.

Since the pastor was not the original pastor, the ceremony was different. The pastor we had met with before sat down and got to know us in two different sessions. He tailored the service to our needs and wants. We had agreed to have parts of the service done in Spanish but the majority of it would be done in English. The replacement pastor divided the ceremony in half, he did all of Johanna's parts in Spanish and all of my parts in English.

Every time there was a break in the action for either prayer or a reading I could feel the unmistakable presence of God over us. I remember when we bowed our heads in prayer during the ceremony I had a vision in my head. The vision was of God watching over the church and his white cloth robe was acting as a blanket over the entire congregation. I can still see that amazingly glorious vision in my head as I am writing this now.

The ring exchange, the lighting of the unity candle and the exchanging of vows flew by at a record setting pace. I think part of it had to do with the fact that the pastor was noticeably nervous. His hands were shaking, he was sweating and he was tripped up by the words more than once. Overall the ceremony was a great success. The outcome was the same as if the original pastor had performed the ceremony. We were united in matrimony in the eyes of God witnessed by our friends and family members.

When we were pronounced husband and wife, both of us were beaming with joy. I turned to Johanna and gave her the three second kiss we had practiced many times in our pre-marital couple's class. We turned and faced the congregation and we were announced as Mr. and Mrs. Wheeler. We walked back up the aisle and exited through the doors to the dressing room.

While in the dressing room we continued to hug and kiss. We discussed our feelings and emotions before and during the ceremony. Our family and friends joined us in this dressing room to wait until the church was cleared out to take pictures. A couple of group shots were taken while we were in the dressing room of everyone in the wedding party and our family members.

Johanna and I wanted pictures with the wedding party and our families while we were still in the church. Most of the people left to go up to the country club for the reception. The longer we stayed the amount of people present in the church shrunk. We said our good byes to our parents and went outside to snap a few more pictures. The photographer told us he was leaving to go up to the reception to take a few pictures and then capture us arriving in our transportation car.

By now we were the only ones left at the church except for a few workers. The hired driver was supposed to be there at a quarter to four. When he was not there we agreed to not take a chance on becoming stranded so we called Maria to come back and pick us up. The Toyota Corolla pulled up and I helped Johanna and her dress get into the passenger side and then I ran around to get into the driver side. While driving away we saw the driver pull up to the church.

Pulling up to the country club we both had to shake off the tiny mishaps that had already occurred telling ourselves to just let it go and have a great time at the reception. We entered the doors and went immediately to the room next to the banquet hall to prepare for our grand entrance. The rest of the wedding party was rounded up and sent to the lobby so that we could all be introduced to music.

Our names were announced by the DJ and we danced in to the Michael Jackson song "Can't Stop til You Get Enough." We found our seats and started to look around at everything and everyone there. The place was beautiful; it looked so elegant and proper. I was glad we had decided on this place for the reception because it was far better than its competition.

We grabbed a quick bite to eat and then we made our rounds to meet and greet everyone. I was so very thankful that I was blessed enough to have all of our closest friends and family together in one room for one night. After touring the room we escaped out the back door to take pictures outside by a lake on the golf course.

Upon our return we took our seats to start dinner. The food was absolutely amazing everything was so delicious. While we were eating I was still in a little bit of shock that we had just been married and my dream had come true. I knew that as people were starting to wind down on the main course we would start the toasts. I still didn't know how or what I was going to say but that I would only speak from my heart.

Scott tapped his wine glass with his spoon to quiet everyone down and draw attention to himself. He pulled his cue cards out from his jacket pocket and began speaking. He had a good speech it was filled with emotion and humor. Then the microphone was passed to the Johanna's sister Michelle who pulled out her note cards and spoke. She also had a wonderful speech and touched on how great Johanna was to her and how excited she was to have a brother like me. In that moment I reflected upon the fact I was so unbelievably grateful for a family like Johanna's. They had taken me into their family and treated me like I had always been a part of the family.

Now the microphone was passed to Johanna. Johanna had a paper filled with notes and this began to make me second guess myself for not having prepared notes. Johanna's speech was a very special and very touching it also had some humor in it as well. Her speech was filled with nothing but heartfelt emotions from start to end. She did announce the fact that I had sold my prized baseball card collection to pay for the wedding and she thanked me for it. I learned later that Jared erupted when she mentioned this. I think it was a cross between the fact that he knew how important my collection was to me and some alcohol he had consumed.

It was now my turn to speak, I had to follow three very good speeches and I didn't have any notes. I spoke from my heart about how much I loved Johanna and how I knew that everything we went through was to arrive at this moment. I told the story about how the pastor didn't show up, only the people behind the scenes knew about this. Then I began telling the story how we had been praying about finding a job elsewhere to be able to buy a house. I let out the good news of how our prayers were answered and we would be moving soon. I concluded by telling everyone how extremely blessed I was to have Johanna as my wife and in my life.

After my speech I offered the microphone to anyone else who wanted to say something but no one came forward. At that time we went to a slideshow I had prepared for our guests. The slideshow started off by showing both Johanna and I as small kids growing up. The next stage was pictures with our friends which were followed by pictures of us with family members. The last part of the slideshow was of us as a couple, from the beginning of our relationship up until the wedding. The cool part was that before I showed pictures of us as a couple I inserted a video clip. The clip was of my proposal to Johanna that Scott had filmed. This was special because all of the people that were not there that night were able to see how I proposed to her.

The rest of the night was filled with the usual wedding events like the bouquet and garter toss, the cake cutting and the money dance. The special part of the evening for me was when Johanna and I shared our first dance. It was a memory that I will never forget. As we started, we looked at each other with ear to ear smiles and our eyes told the whole story of how much we loved each other. As we danced around the dance floor we talked to each other about how happy we were and how much we loved each other. This was a nice moment to reflect on how beautifully everything was going.

Once we finished our first dance as a married couple Johanna brought her father out onto the dance floor for the father daughter dance. I know this was a very special moment for both of them. I could just imagine myself in Reyes' shoes and how he must have felt that his little girl was all grown up now.

After their dance was done I went and brought my mother out on the dance floor. My mom doesn't know how to dance but I wasn't going to let that stop her from sharing this moment with me. As I danced with my mom we could tell how happy each other was. My mom was happy I found a perfect wife in Johanna and I was happy because my mom was happy.

I remember a couple of days before the wedding my mom had called and I was lying on the bed with Johanna. I answered the phone call and put my mother on speaker phone. My mom wanted to express how unbelievably happy she was I met a girl like Johanna. She couldn't praise Johanna enough about how she had brought me to the Lord. My mom went on by saying that my life could have been very different if I would have married one of my girlfriends from the past. The thing that was so special is Johanna was listening in on what my mom was telling me and my mom had no idea.

As the reception started to wind down we were a little glad because we were exhausted. We all started to pick everything up and had a moment to reflect on what a fabulous and blessed day it had been. A few minor hiccups but with God's help we made it through it all. Johanna and I got into the car with her dad and he drove us to the Airtel Plaza Hotel in Van Nuys. We laid in the hotel bed talking about how everything went and if it was how we thought it was going to be. We reflected about how much planning, money and preparation had gone into one single day. It truly was amazing.

The next morning we met and had breakfast with Rubio, his girlfriend, Kevin, Lindsey and Connors in the hotel. After breakfast we took them to the airport and then returned home. Once home we began opening all of our gifts from the wedding. It felt good to know there were so many people that cared for us out there. We had asked for money to be able to help us in our efforts to purchase a home. We also asked for gift cards because we were moving and needed things for our apartment. All of our bags were packed and we left for the airport that night for our honeymoon.

13

Fresh Outlook

Our flight left around eleven thirty at night for the Dominican Republic. When we arrived in the Dominican Republic, for our honeymoon, we felt such an extreme sense of relaxation. I am not sure if it was that we were so far away from everyone and everything or if it was the fact that this was the first real time we had spent alone as a couple. Whatever the case, it was blissful. Our hotel accommodations were excellent, the food was exquisite and you couldn't ask for better weather.

We went on a guided tour to an island off of the coast and on the way we drove through much of the region. The people live in poverty and are very simplistic people. This time I saw the countryside with the knowledge of God in me and it was a constant reminder of how blessed we are in our own lives. Our honeymoon was the greatest vacation I have ever been on and I was fortunate enough to spend it with my beautiful wife who is also my best friend.

Returning back home was bittersweet because we were back to our lives where we couldn't be so carefree, not to mention that I had to return to work. Being back home was good in the sense that it allowed me to be grateful and thankful for everything around me. I realized how important our families are in our lives and how special the bond with them really is. I was also thankful to God for the blessing of my new job that was quickly approaching.

I only worked at Kaiser West Los Angeles for another three weeks after my return from my honeymoon. This gave me enough time to make a training guide for the people that were covering me and for the new person they were going to hire. It also gave me time to say my goodbyes. I did enjoy my time while at that facility because it gave me insight into how the hospital was run and how to get things accomplished on a much larger scale.

The next couple of weekends we had a couple of yard sales to raise money for the move and to clear space. One weekend we had a yard sale at my parents and then the next down at Johanna's parent's house. Between the two separate yard sales we were blessed enough to raise around six hundred dollars. Not only did we have a fun time putting on the sales we also helped people by donating the clothes that we did not sell to the homeless.

The time went by so fast and before I knew it we were packing for the move. The weekend of the move came. Saturday we spent the day packing everything up. We prepared everything to be loaded up. Johanna's room was now virtually empty and it started to hit me we were really doing this. The time I spent in her parent's house was very brief in the sense of time but I would not trade it for the world.

The next morning we woke up ready for the move. As I went into the kitchen Reyes wanted to sit me down and talk to me for a minute. I really was not prepared for what he was going to tell me. We both walked to the living room and sat down on opposite couches so we could talk to each other face to face. He wanted to thank me for my coming in to their house and helping out after his surgery. He expressed to me that over the past months of my living there he really got to learn a lot about me. He learned what type of man I was and how strong my love for Johanna was.

Reyes also wanted to warn me about living on our own and he wanted me to take care of his daughter. I felt so many warm feelings inside when he was speaking to me because I knew the person that I was now and how good I felt inside. I thought to myself how far I had come from who I was until now. I am so thankful that Johanna brought me to the Lord and I was saved. I now felt confident that I was who I was always meant to be and I felt proud of my journey. I knew the confidence that Reyes had in me was all through his faith in God.

When Chase and his dad, Andy, arrived we were all ready to pack up the truck and trailer and be on our way. We made a stop in Palmdale to load up some more furniture and eat some lunch. From Palmdale we left with a convoy of Chase and Andy, me, Johanna and Michelle and bringing up the rear was Maria and Reyes. My parents left about an hour after we did and stopped to pick up my grandma so that she could make the journey as well.

When we arrived at our new apartment we began unpacking all of our stuff from the truck and placing it in its intended spot. Chase's mom, Kelly, and brother, Chance, stopped by to lend a hand in our move. When it was time for everyone to leave there were plenty of boxes that had not been put away, but the majority of the stuff was in place. We thanked everyone for helping and said goodbye to our parents. Our first night in our place felt quiet and a little lonely. As we laid in bed we prayed. We gave thanks for such a beautiful day and everything that came throughout the day. We prayed for a safe journey home for everyone who helped us and gave thanks for such great people to surround ourselves with.

The next day was my first day at work. Johanna ironed my clothes for the day, packed my lunch and made me breakfast. As I sat enjoying my breakfast I thought how lucky I was to have such a perfect wife in my life and to think I could have missed out on everything good in my life. I left for work and was amazed at the scenery throughout my drive. I have heard people call Tehachapi "God's country" and it is so true. There was no traffic on my way to work which was such a pleasant change of pace. I used to dread my drive home when I worked at Kaiser West Los Angeles but now the drive home was a breeze as well.

When I came in the door Johanna was cooking dinner and the house was filled with a delicious aroma. We sat down for dinner, blessed the food and our day and then began to enjoy her wonderful cooking. Now because Johanna was still enrolled in Mission College in Sylmar she would still have to make the commute until the semester ended. After dinner she gathered her things to make the journey to her parent's house. She went out the door and would not return for three days.

I wasn't prepared for how much I would miss her. I woke up the next morning to an empty spot next to me in bed. I had to make my own breakfast and pack my own lunch. The apartment just didn't feel right, it was lonely. I went out the door to work and called Johanna to talk to on my drive to work. I told her how much I missed her but I reassured her that this was only a temporary thing. If we could get through these next couple of months with this schedule then God would continue to bless us and open doors for us.

I am able to look at my life and be so thankful I am where I am. I am working towards where I want to be in my life spiritually. My relationship with God is so great and by having such a great relationship with Him has also blessed my other relationships. I am constantly striving towards improving upon my marriage and with God in the center it makes such a huge difference. Everything around me is a constant reminder of how glorious and almighty God is. I can't even imagine where I would be without God's interventions. I could have taken a thousand different avenues in my life but none of them would have brought me to where I am without the good Lord in my life.

14

My Prayers and Thoughts

Prayer

Prayer is a key aspect in forming a relationship with God. It is very important to stay connected with God through prayer. I also learned that even though I pray with my wife I need to have a personal relationship with God and spend some time with him alone. The time I spend with God is usually through prayer throughout the day. I have had many prayers since becoming a Christian but none have been bigger than the prayer I say for my dad. I always pray for the Lord to soften his heart and to take away the negativity he has for Christianity and

God. My dad is a very smart man and very firmly set in his ways of being a non-believer. He is a factual kind of guy and doesn't rely on faith for much of anything. I am not sure why he is so against believing in God, maybe he had a bad experience or got some bad information.

He doesn't know the affect this has had on the people that love him. I know my mom has worried about this for a long time but now she is more worried because of my dad's age. Our family is a very distant family and we don't talk about personal feelings unless we are confronted head on with them. My dad has always been there for me and would do anything for anyone of his children. This is why it hurts so much when I think he won't be joining me in heaven.

I don't think my dad understands the importance of making the commitment to God. He is probably thinking he will make the decision on his death bed, but what if he doesn't get that chance? My mom loves her husband and it eats me to see her so sad about something that is able to be changed. I guarantee the decision to give your life to Jesus Christ will be the most important of his or anyone's life. I can only demonstrate how I feel since turning to the Lord through my words and hope being his son he will trust me. Ultimately the decision is his to make, I can't force him or anyone for that matter. Hopefully he will have a glimpse of what I have gone through to get where I am today and will want to see it and feel it for himself. Let me tell you as someone who has made the decision to become a man of faith, the decision was a no brainer.

I have always understood the importance of family but didn't always find it necessarily to be true all of the time. I now pray every night that my family is kept safe and are protected. The power of prayer is so powerful and just by praying for someone you can feel your heart grow closer to that person. I was also blessed to be able to be a part of Johanna's family. Their family is a very close knit family and they have shown me a glimpse of how I want my own family to be. I want to attend church as a family and be able to have my kids come to me with personal feelings and questions. I am so unbelievably lucky to have so much love through my family and my in-laws. I thank God in my prayers for my family and for Johanna's family, they both are truly blessings.

I have heard testimonies in church that have made me cry. I've seen miracles of God first hand in my own life that make me value how short of a time we really do have on earth. The important thing is to not try to get everything out of life on earth. Instead the goal is to prepare yourself to enter utopia that God has made for us in heaven. This can be accomplished by walking with God on earth and doing His will. Not living for the moment or living for you but to live for Him.

I do pray to God when I have needs whether they are immediate or in the future. It is important to pray to God for things in your life that you need, but make sure you also discern whether they really are needs or just wants. The other important thing to remember is when God answers your prayers for needs you give Him thanks. God is an awesome provider and it feels so good to be the recipient of His blessings because it brings joy and happiness. God will always look out for you if you are looking out for Him, make sure you are doing His will and not your own. He will provide for you in times of need and show you the light at the end of the tunnel.

Being thankful for all God does needs to be done whenever you get the chance. You will never be able to thank God for everything, because there is just not enough time but you can try. Anytime you get a chance to thank Him do so. Don't just thank Him for things you pray for either, there is much more we don't pray for we need to be thankful for as well. I always start my prayers at night off by saying "Lord thank you for another beautiful day." This can be done throughout the day, sometime when you are driving thank God for giving you the ability to see his glory all around you. You will be amazed at the feeling you get when you give thanks, it brings a smile to my face whenever I give God thanks.

I have received so many blessings from God over such a short period of time it is unbelievable. A non believer might just say I am lucky, which would be true because I am lucky to have found God. I am so graced for all of the blessings God has bestowed upon me. I know that He will continue to bless me as long as I carry out His word. My works in this life are all for Him. Sometimes it is easy to lose track of this goal but it is important to stay on the path He has for us. It is such a great feeling to be awarded such blessings and makes me think about how great His kingdom is and how blissful I will be in heaven.

Overall my relationship with God has improved every facet of my life by one-hundred percent. My life is not dark and gloomy but filled with light and glory. My future is no longer cloudy, it is filled with hope. I know with God at the center of my life I will enjoy a wonderful life and be able to flourish with those around me. I feel everyone should be able to have an insight of what the Lord has done for me.

I have heard powerful testimonies that have touched me and caused me to look at my own life and to be thankful for what I have. I want my testimony to do the same thing for everyone who picks up this book. I feel if I can reach one person through the words I have written than I have done what God has asked me to do. I believe I was called upon by the Lord to change people's lives through my book. I was given the ability and the gift to be able to reach out to people who I don't even know, who read this book. I also feel that in my own community there are people I was called upon to help them to find the Lord.

"You have been chosen by God himself—you are priests of the King, you are holy and pure, you are God's very own—all this so that you may show to others how God called you out of the darkness into His wonderful light"

-1 Peter 2:9

Thoughts

As the world falls apart around us God provides the only white light of hope. All He wants is to love us and take care of us. He has unconditional love for all of his children all you have to do is to accept Him into your heart. This is the best possible gift that anyone could ever receive. Having faith in Him and following His word will change your life beyond a point you could never have ever imagined possible.

In James 4:10 it says "Humble yourselves before the Lord and He shall lift you up." This is such a great reward. Being lifted by the Lord will be such an awesome life changing transformation. Take a look at your own life and make the choice to open up your heart and receive Jesus Christ into your heart. All you have to do is be ready to come to the Lord and accept Jesus Christ as your Lord and Savior. God will provide, protect, heal, love, forgive and make your overall life experience on earth a wonderful time. The more clearly we understand Him, the more we will find His love irresistible. As we begin to experience His love, our own lives will begin to make more sense.

I hope this book has shed a little bit of light on the effects of accepting the Lord into my own life has had. My life went from being an out of control downward spiral to the complete opposite now. I used to think the more accomplishments or the more material things I had is what made people want to be like me. Now I know I want to live my life as God wants me to and people will notice me as a pillar in the community. I hope my story has helped you understand why it is necessary to change and that it is possible to change. No matter where you are in your walk of life you can come to God. He is waiting for you with open arms to pour out His blessings on you.

I have been lucky enough to have been touched by an angel and been brought into the light. My experience has changed my life forever for the better. My life has been blessed in so many ways since I opened my heart up to Jesus. I have been blessed with a beautiful wife, a great job and a lifetime full of happiness and peace. I saw a saying one time on a license plate frame and it is so true it said "No God – No Peace" on the top and on the bottom it said "Know God – Know Peace."

My plan was to show you through my testimony that the world without God is pretty ugly and difficult. I tried to open up the eyes of the reader with real life situations and circumstances. Remember God is life and God forgives. This is the truth and I am so glad I am able to live in God's glory. In closing I want you to remember and take a long look at the most famous Bible verse of all time.

John 3:16

For God so loved the world that he gave his only begotten son, so whoever shall believeth in him shall not perish but have everlasting life.

www.ingramcontent.com/pod-product-compliance
Ingram Content Group UK Ltd.
Pitfield, Milton Keynes, MK11 3LW, UK
UKHW041946190726
13854UKWH00004B/1822

9 780557 490516